U0061531

中 華 書 局

回 歸
「一國兩制」的初心
——「一國兩制」漫談

（第三版）
(3rd Edition)

The Original Intent of "One Country, Two Systems"

An Informal Chat on "One Country, Two Systems"

蕭平 / 著

Xiao Ping

回歸「一國兩制」的初心
——「一國兩制」漫談

（第三版）
(3rd Edition)

The Original Intent of "One Country, Two Systems"
An Informal Chat on "One Country, Two Systems"

蕭 平 ——— 著
Xiao Ping

出版 / 中華書局（香港）有限公司

香港北角英皇道 499 號北角工業大廈 1 樓 B 室

電話：(852) 2137 2338　傳真：(852) 2713 8202

電子郵件：info@chunghwabook.com.hk

網址：http://www.chunghwabook.com.hk

發行 / 香港聯合書刊物流有限公司

新界荃灣德士古道 220-248 號荃灣工業中心 16 樓

電話：(852) 2150 2100　傳真：(852) 2407 3062

電子郵件：info@suplogistics.com.hk

印刷 / 美雅印刷製本有限公司

香港觀塘榮業街 6 號海濱工業大廈 4 字樓 A 室

版次 / 2020 年 5 月第 1 版

2023 年 4 月第 3 版第 2 次印刷

@ 2020 2023 中華書局（香港）有限公司

規格 / 32 開（210mm×148mm）

ISBN / 978-988-8809-42-4

目 錄

Contents

回歸「一國兩制」的初心
——「一國兩制」漫談

導言：回首二十五年 讀懂「一國兩制」

　　香港回歸祖國已經二十五年，「一國兩制」經歷了實踐的檢驗。站在這個時點上回首過去，我們對「一國兩制」有了更加深切的感悟。習近平主席在香港發表重要講話，鄭重宣示「一國兩制」方針必須長期堅持，回答了全面準確貫徹「一國兩制」方針的重大理論和現實問題，為深刻認識「一國兩制」的理論邏輯和實踐規律，提供了指引。

　　作為前無古人的制度探索，「一國兩制」實踐取得舉世公認的成功，同時也遇到一些干擾和衝擊，受各種內外複雜因素影響，香港局勢一度出現嚴峻局面。中央適時出手撥亂反正，制定香港國安法，完善特區選舉制度，採取一系列標本兼治的舉措，推動香港實現由亂到治的重大轉折，「一國兩制」實踐重回正軌。

　　但凡新的探索難免有不盡人意的波折，「一國兩制」事業也是在一次次迎接挑戰、解決問題的過程中破浪前行的，得與失，經驗與教訓，都是寶貴的財富。回首二十五年，我們對「一國兩制」的要義看得更加清晰，它至少包含以下幾點：

其一，維護國家主權、安全和發展利益是最高原則。「一國兩制」是國家統一和國家治理的制度安排，首要目標是國家統一。基本法序言寫明，設立特別行政區並實行「一國兩制」，是為了維護國家的統一和領土完整，保持香港的繁榮和穩定。中共十八大報告指出，維護國家主權、安全和發展利益，維護香港長期繁榮穩定，是「一國兩制」的根本宗旨。香港享有特殊制度安排的前提，是必須扛起維護國家安全和國家利益的憲制責任，守住習近平主席劃定的「三條底線」。

其二，憲法和基本法共同構成特別行政區的憲制基礎。憲法是國家的根本法、最高法，基本法是依據憲法制定的，不能拋開憲法講基本法，特區不存在脫離國家憲法的「憲制」和「法治」。這樣的憲制基礎和憲制秩序，要求香港實行的制度必須與國家主體實行的制度相協調、相適應。特區政府和香港居民必須遵從憲法的精神，尊重和維護中國共產黨的領導，尊重和維護國家的政治制度及體制。同時維護基本法的權威，確保基本法各項規定的落實。

　　其三，中央全面管治權與特區高度自治權相統一。主權與治權不可分割，中國政府對香港恢復行使主權之時也就擁有了對香港的全面管治權。特區的高度自治不是固有的，而是中央授權的結果。全面管治權是高度自治權的源頭，兩者統一銜接才能把特區治理好。特區政府向中央政府負責，接受中央政府的監督和問責。中央對特區政治體制、政治制度等重大問題有最終決定權，特區自治範圍內的事務由特區負責。

　　其四，堅持行政主導的特別行政區政治體制。這一點是上一點的延伸。香港回歸後重新納入國家治理體系，特區治理是國家治理的組成部分，特區的政治體制必須與國家主體的政治體制有效銜接。香港實行行政主導體制，是由我國單一制國家結構和特區作為地方行政區的憲制地位決定的，是行政長官對中央負責的有效方式。香港的政制發展必須有利於落實行政主導，確保行政長官在特區治理中的核心地位和權威，提高施政效能。

　　其五，必須落實「愛國者治港」。「愛國者治港」是「港人治港」的界限。基本法明確要求行政長官等公職人員必須宣誓擁護《中華人民共和國香港特別行政區基本法》，效忠中華人民共和國香港特別行政區。治港者必須具有牢固的國家觀念，特區的選舉制度必須確保進入管治架構的人，都是堅定的愛國者。守護好管治權，就是守護香港繁榮穩定，守護香港居民的切身利益。

其六，保持香港的獨特地位和優勢。實行「一國兩制」，就是要在解決統一問題的前提下，最大限度保留香港的特色和優勢。香港背靠祖國，聯通世界，具有不可替代的獨特作用。融入國家發展大局，以香港所長服務國家所需，進而實現自身更大發展，符合國家的發展戰略，符合國家和香港的根本利益和長遠利益。香港應該在民族復興的進程中，與祖國人民共擔責任，共享榮光。

以上各點相互聯繫、內在統一，從中可以看出一個共同特徵，那就是先有「一國」後有「兩制」，沒有「一國」就沒有「兩制」。「一國兩制」是在國家主體堅持社會主義制度的前提下制定的政策。也就是說，內地是主體，內地實行的制度是前提，沒有主體和前提，「一國兩制」就是空中樓閣。鄧小平先生一語破的，他說：「我們搞的是有中國特色的社會主義，所以才制定『一國兩制』的政策，才可以允許兩種制度存在。」「沒有中國共產黨，沒有中國的社會主義，誰能夠制定這樣的政策？」

「一國兩制」的獨特性在於，國家主體的社會主義與局部地區的資本主義並行不悖，由國家主體提供依託，以特殊的制度安排保持局部地區的特殊性。所以習近平主席說：「『一國』原則愈堅固，『兩制』優勢愈彰顯。」理解「一國兩制」方針，把握這一點最為緊要。

回首過去是為了面向未來。未來「一國兩制」更長的路應該怎樣走？最為關鍵的一點，就是按照習近平主席的要求，全面準確貫徹「一國兩制」方針。何謂「全面準確」？那就是不論「一國兩制」在實踐中遇到什麼挑戰、如何發展演進，其中要義必須始終堅持，一以貫之。

江天遼闊，前程錦繡。二十五年風雨兼程，香港步入了由治及興的新階段。堅守初心，與時俱進，香港定能續寫「一國兩制」的新篇章。

開篇的話：
回歸「一國兩制」的初心

　　「不忘初心，方得始終。」這是一個樸素的真理。香港「一國兩制」遇到種種衝突和挑戰，最根本的原因是對「一國兩制」的認知和落實未能做到全面準確，偏離了它的初心。因此，尋根溯源，回歸初心，對於今日之香港很有必要。

　　歷史的時針撥回到 1949 年 10 月。解放軍吹響「解放全中國」的號角，揮師南下，風捲殘雲，卻在深圳河畔勒住戰馬。以戰爭的方式趕走英國殖民者，復疆雪恥，沒有人懷疑解放軍的戰鬥力。但中共中央定下了「長期打算」的方針，香港問題暫時擱置。歷史證明這個方針是英明的。後來在新中國被西方長期封鎖的年代，香港成為中國與外部聯繫的通道。再後來在內地改革開放的進程中，香港又成為助力國家發展的重要引擎。

　　事實上，中國政府解決港澳和台灣問題、實現國家完全統一的意志從未動搖。需要考慮的不是要不要統一，而是以什麼方式統一，哪種方式代價最小、能讓更多人接受。鄧小平先生講得很清楚：「中國面臨的實際問題就是用什麼方式才能解決香港問題，用什麼方式才能解決台灣問題。只能有兩種方式，一種是和平方式，一種是非和平方式。」「香港繼續保持繁榮，根本上取決於中國收回香港後，在中國的管轄之下，實行適合於香港的政策。」

什麼才是「適合於香港的政策」呢？經過深思熟慮，鄧小平開創性地提出了「一個國家、兩種制度」的偉大構想，從而為中國也為國際社會解決歷史遺留問題提供了一個全新而又可行的方案，改變了歷史上收復失地大都兵戎相見的定式。這是中國對國家統一和國家治理模式的大膽探索，對人類政治文明的巨大貢獻。

「一國兩制」最初是為解決台灣問題提出來的，卻首先在香港落地，這是歷史的機緣選擇。回歸二十多年來，「一國兩制」由構想變為現實，得到國際社會的普遍認可，香港整體上保持了繁榮穩定，證明「一國兩制」是行得通、辦得到、得人心的。1997 年美國《財富》雜誌曾斷言「香港已死」，多年後不得不承認「我們錯了」。

「一國兩制」是關於國家統一和國家治理的方針，香港回歸前主要解決統一的問題，香港回歸後主要用於特區的治理。習近平主席説：「一個不知道自己來路的民族，是沒有出路的民族。」回溯歷史有助於解釋和解決今天的問題。比如，為什麼選擇「一國兩制」而不是「一國一制」？為什麼説中央對香港有全面管治權？為什麼是行政主導而不是三權分立？香港回歸後什麼都沒變嗎？2047 後還有「一國兩制」嗎？為什麼中央出手制定香港國安法？為什麼必須堅持「愛國者治港」？等等。這些問題搞清楚了，澄清似是而非的誤解和混淆視聽的曲解，就知道該堅持和完善什麼，該糾正和摒棄什麼，「一國兩制」之路就會行穩致遠，愈走愈寬。

　　大道至簡。讓我們一起步入系列漫談，梳理「一國兩制」的脈絡，重温「一國兩制」的初心。

為什麼選擇「一國兩制」?

　　為什麼選擇「一國兩制」?還有別的制度選擇嗎?中國政府確定以「一國兩制」方針收回和治理香港,是出於怎樣的動機呢?

　　九七回歸後,香港可以實行「一國一制」嗎?從法理上講是完全可以的。主權與治權緊密相連,中國政府對香港恢復行使主權,就意味着可以行使治權。按照憲法,中國共產黨是中國唯一的執政黨,執政半徑理所當然覆蓋香港。因此,如果在終結港英管治後徹底「另起爐灶」,把內地的制度引入香港,如管治內地省市般管治香港,是完全符合主權原則和國際慣例的。

　　但中央政府沒有那樣做,而是把香港設立為特別行政區,以授權的方式,實行「一國兩制」,「港人治港」,高度自治。為此,全國人大專門制定了《中華人民共和國香港特別行政區基本法》,對中央與特區關係、香港居民的權利與義務，以及特區自治範圍內的事務做出明確規定，並承諾五十年不變。

為什麼可以「一國一制」卻要「一國兩制」？這是「充分照顧到香港的歷史和現實情況」（鄧小平語）做出的政治決斷。這個決斷各方都能接受，它的根本出發點就是，在解決統一問題的前提下，最大限度保留香港的特色和優勢，令香港在回歸後繼續保持繁榮穩定。

原全國政協主席李瑞環給港澳地區全國政協委員講過一個「茶壺的故事」。話說一位老太太把家中一把上百年的紫砂壺拿到市場去賣，開價五錢銀子。一位買主很懂行，見壺內有茶山（經年歷久形成的茶垢），知道是難得的好東西，願出價三兩，隨後回家去取銀子。老太太心想，一把舊壺給這麼多錢，裏面有垢實在不好意思，於是就把茶山刮淨了。稍後買主回來，一看茶山沒了，掉頭就走不買了。這個故事意味深長，道出了中央對香港價值的珍視，可以從中體會「一國兩制」的良苦用心。

打個譬喻，香港好像一個遊子，離家太久了，疏離感是難免的，對家裏的規矩和粗茶淡飯難以適應。因此，保留原有的社會制度和生活方式不變，既是大多數港人所願，也與中央考慮香港問題的出發點相契合。上世紀八九十年代的香港，已經是區域性國際金融、貿易、航運中心，獨特的營商環境、法治規則和國際聯繫，是任何一個內地城市都不具備的。如果實行「一國一制」，中國只是多了一個幾百萬人口的現代化城市，卻可能失去一顆獨具特色的「東方之珠」。新中國成立後尤其改革開放後，香港以其獨特的優勢，助力國家發展，彌補國家短板，發揮了難以替代的作用。保留原有的社會制度和生活方式，不僅有利於香港繼續繁榮穩定，也可以令香港為國家未來發展做出更大的貢獻，可謂利國利港，一舉雙得。用鄧小平的話說，「香港的繁榮和穩定同中國的發展戰略有着密切的關聯」，「保持香港的繁榮穩定是符合中國的切身利益的」。

為什麼説「一國兩制」是中國特色社會主義的重要內容？

　　基本法規定香港回歸後不實行社會主義制度，保持原有的資本主義制度五十年不變。可鄧小平先生説，「一國兩制」是中國特色社會主義「很重要的一個內容」。這該怎麼理解呢？

　　鄧小平道出了一個事實，即，因為是搞中國特色社會主義，才能做出「一國兩制」這一特殊的制度安排。什麼是中國特色社會主義？簡單説就是「社會主義」加「中國特色」，既堅持社會主義基本原理，又立足國情、走符合中國自身實際的社會主義道路。改革開放，社會主義市場經濟，多種所有制共同發展，多種分配方式並存等等，與此前既有的社會主義模式有所不同，都是中國特色社會主義的產物。同樣，「一國兩制」也是中國共產黨從國家發展大局及香港歷史和現實情況出發，實事求是創造出來的，是與傳統意義上的社會主義看似不相容的新制度模式。鄧小平説：「我們的社會主義制度是有中國特色的社會主義制度，這個特色，很重要的一個內容就是對香港、澳門、台灣問題的處理，就是『一國兩制』。」「我們搞的是有中國特色的社會主義，所以才制定『一國兩制』的政策，才可以允許兩種制度存在。」

　　強調「一國兩制」是中國特色社會主義的重要內容，有三個突出的含義。第一，「兩制」是有主次的，源頭活水是內地。「一國兩制」是在國家主體堅持社會主義制度的前提下制定的政策，內地是主體，內地實行的制度是前提，沒有主體和前提，就沒有「一國兩制」。第二，特區的制度要與國家主體的制度相協調。特區的制度不同於獨立政治實體的主權制度，不能與內地的社會主義制度對抗，而應適應協調、和諧共處。第三，內地一制不變是香港一制不變的保證。鄧小平一語破的：「要保持香港五十年繁榮和穩定，五十年以後也繁榮和穩定，就要保持中國共產黨領導下的社會主義制度。」

　　強調「一國兩制」是中國特色社會主義的重要內容，不是要用內地的社會主義取代香港的資本主義，恰恰是要讓香港更好的發展，同時助力國家發展，與國家一起發展。建設中國特色社會主義需要借鑒世界文明的優秀成果，香港在這方面可以發揮重要作用。實行「一國兩

制」與國家發展戰略是一致的，鄧小平説：「中國的主體
必須是社會主義，但允許國內某些區域實行資本主義制
度。」「在小範圍內容許資本主義存在，更有利於發展社
會主義。」

　　中國共產黨是中國特色社會主義的領導者，當然也
是「一國兩制」的領導者。在中國共產黨的領導下，社會
主義可以包容資本主義，將「一國兩制」視作我國國家制
度和國家治理體系的一個顯著優勢，確定為新時代堅持
和發展中國特色社會主義的一項基本方略。

為什麼要「摸着石頭過河」？

　　「摸着石頭過河」，這是內地改革開放之初鼓勵探索的一句口頭禪。「一國兩制」前無古人，要讓這一全新的制度體系順利落地並發揮預想的效用，至少在初始階段也要「摸着石頭過河」。

　　2019年10月召開的中共十九屆四中全會指出，「『一國兩制』是黨領導人民實現祖國和平統一的一項重要制度，是中國特色社會主義的一個偉大創舉」。這是對「一國兩制」重要作用和歷史地位的高度肯定。

　　其實，對於「一國兩制」，從不同的角度有不同的表述。就難易程度而論，十六屆四中全會稱它是中國共產黨治國理政的「嶄新課題」，十七大又稱是「重大課題」。就執政思路而論，十九大確定了新時代堅持和發展中國特色社會主義的十四條基本方略，堅持「一國兩制」是其中的一條。就性質特徵而論，十九屆四中全會列出了我國國家制度和國家治理體系十三個方面的顯著優勢，堅持「一國兩制」也是其中之一。

不同的表述串起了這樣一條邏輯鏈：因為是偉大創舉，所以前無古人，所以是嶄新課題；因為是治國方略，所以屬重要制度，所以需不斷完善；因為有顯著優勢，所以充滿自信，所以要長期堅持。

九七回歸前，「一國兩制」沒有可以借鑒的現成經驗。國民黨統治大陸時，中共曾經在湘贛、陝北等地成立蘇維埃紅色政權，建政立法，還發行獨立的貨幣。儘管「解放區的天是晴朗的天」，但在當時的統治者眼裏，那是不合法的，以至要重兵圍剿，一力「安內」，與回歸後香港在國家保護和支持下的高度自治完全不是一回事。世界上一些享有某種自治權的地方，都與它所在的國家實行同樣的社會制度，也與「一國兩制」不是一回事。

中共十六大闡述了中國共產黨自成立之日起經歷的兩次歷史方位的轉變。一次是新中國成立時，由為奪取政權而奮鬥的黨變為掌握政權並長期執政的黨；另一次是改革開放後，由在封閉的計劃經濟條件下領導國家建設的黨，變為在開放的市場經濟條件下領導國家建設的黨。仔細想一想，香港回歸也意味着中共執政方式的一

次歷史性轉變，即從單一社會主義條件下領導國家建設
的黨，變為在國家主體實行社會主義、局部地區實行資
本主義條件下領導國家建設的黨。這個轉變或許不能同
前兩個相提並論，卻實實在在地構成對中共執政的全新
考驗。

　　同樣的，對香港來說，「一國兩制」也是全新的課
題。鄧小平說：「『一國兩制』是個新事物，有很多我
們預料不到的事情。」誰都不是神仙，要熟悉「一國兩
制」，中央與特區都需要一個學習的過程。由於經驗不
足，由於新情況新問題層出不窮，在五十年乃至更長的
演進中，「一國兩制」遇到波折在所難免，要在探索中逐
步把握實踐規律。隨着實踐拓展和認識深化，「一國兩
制」制度體系會不斷完善，前行的路就會愈走愈穩、愈
走愈寬。

為什麼「一國兩制」
要講兩句話？

　　「一國兩制」是個完整的概念。從字面看，前面是「一國」，後面是「兩制」，道出了它們之間的主次關係，體現了兩者不可分割。要準確定義「一國兩制」，就必須講兩句話、兩個方面，把兩者的關係講清楚。

　　基本法序言寫明，實行「一國兩制」，是為了維護國家的統一和領土完整，保持香港的繁榮和穩定。但過去很長一段時間裏，對「一國兩制」的宣介不夠完整，講「港人治港」、高度自治多，講中央權力、「兩制」關係少，強調中央不干預特區內部事務，強調香港遇到問題的時候祖國內地是堅強後盾，「兩制」是「井水不犯河水」。這些講法並不錯，但不全面，久而久之容易導致重一制輕另一制，不利於樹立正確的「一國兩制」價值觀。

　　「井水不犯河水」的原意是，內地不在香港搞社會主義，香港也不要把資本主義搬到內地來，不能解讀為「兩制」互不相干。別有用心者以「反干預」之名排斥中央權力，割裂「兩制」，抗拒「一國」，這是回歸後香港出現的背離「一國兩制」亂象的典型表現。

內地與香港、中央與特區，是緊密相連的整體，維護國家主權、安全、發展利益是「一國兩制」方針的最高原則。有心人會注意到，自中共十八大以後，「一國兩制」的表述都講兩句話了，即從國家和香港兩個方面把它講完整。例如「根本宗旨是維護國家主權、安全、發展利益，維護香港、澳門長期繁榮穩定」（十八大）；「依法行使中央權力，依法保障高度自治」（十八屆四中全會）；「必須把維護中央對香港、澳門特別行政區全面管治權和保障特別行政區高度自治權有機結合起來」（十九大）。這些表述有一個共同的特徵，就是國家在前，香港在後。也就是説，「兩制」是「一國」之下的「兩制」，實施「一國兩制」必須把國家安全和利益放在第一位。

中央一再強調，貫徹「一國兩制」方針，既要「堅定不移」，還要「全面準確」。在香港回歸祖國二十周年慶典上，習近平主席對「一國」與「兩制」的關係做了透徹説明。他説，「一國」是實行「兩制」的前提和基礎，「兩制」從屬和派生於「一國」，並統一於「一國」之內。「一國」是根，根深才能葉茂；「一國」是本，本固才能枝榮。習主席這番話，是理解「一國」與「兩制」關係的邏輯起點，是必要的正本清源。

推而廣之，「堅持『一國』原則和尊重『兩制』差異」「發揮祖國內地堅強後盾作用和提高特別行政區自身競爭力」「堅守『一國』之本，善用『兩制』之利」，這些說法都是根與葉、源與流的堅守和拓展。

鄧小平曾經諄諄告誡港人，社會主義的內地是「一國兩制」的主體和保證，「這是個前提，沒有這個前提不行」，「改變了中國共產黨領導下的具有中國特色的社會主義制度，香港會是怎樣？香港的繁榮和穩定也會吹的」，「不講兩個方面，『一國兩制』幾十年不變就行不通了」。

為什麼回歸前的香港不是殖民地？

九七前，英國視香港為殖民地，所謂「海外屬土」不過是殖民地的另一種稱謂。但香港其實不是殖民地，只是英國人在這裏實行了殖民統治。區分這一點十分重要，有助於理解香港回歸祖國的涵義，認清港英搞「光榮撤退」的用心，看穿「港獨」主張的荒謬。

在英國殖民者眼中，香港島和九龍半島「永久割讓」，英國理所當然擁有主權。新界雖為租借，但租期長達九十九年，以「日不落帝國」的淫威對付積貧積弱的舊中國，歸還與否無需考慮。毫無疑問，當年的英國政府完全是以宗主國的身份，按殖民地模式經營和管治香港的。

但這只是他們的一廂情願。辛亥革命後歷屆中國政府均不承認「割讓」香港的不平等條約，從未放棄對香港的領土主權。中華人民共和國在恢復聯合國合法席位後不久，即致函聯合國非殖民化委員會，鄭重聲明：

「香港、澳門是屬於歷史上遺留下來的帝國主義強加於中國的一系列不平等條約的結果。香港和澳門是被英國和葡萄牙當局佔領的中國領土的一部分,解決香港、澳門問題完全是屬於中國主權範圍內的問題,根本不屬於通常的『殖民地』範疇。」1972 年 11 月,聯合國大會以九十九票對五票,通過了將香港、澳門從殖民地名單上刪除的決議。中國此舉是對歷史事實的確認,更是對國家主權的堅定維護。

二戰後興起了一波殖民地獨立潮。一些殖民地在脫離宗主國的同時,也改變了過往的國家關係,宣佈獨立,成為新的主權國家。但香港不同,香港是待收回的國土,主權始終屬於中國,不存在爭取主權和民族獨立的問題。把香港從聯合國殖民地名單中拿掉,杜絕了主權爭議,為香港回歸祖國掃清了可能的障礙。所以,無論《中英聯合聲明》還是基本法,寫的都不是「收回主權」或「主權回歸」,而是「恢復行使主權」。基本法序言及第 1 條開宗明義:「香港自古以來就是中國的領土」,「香港特別行政區是中華人民共和國不可分離的部分」。

英國是老牌帝國,每每在結束殖民統治前大搞所謂「光榮撤退」,製造族羣對立,倉促開放選舉,導致社會動盪、政府弱勢，這樣就可以繼續維持宗主國的影響力。港英政府在回歸前的過渡期也使出這一伎倆，驟然加速選舉進程。最後一任港督彭定康到任三個月就拋出激進政改方案，並得意地宣稱香港正在經歷「一個政治城市邁向民主的過程」，一手毀掉了立法局直接過渡為特區立法會的「直通車」。過往百多年不搞民主，現在忽然要「還政於民」，令人不禁要問，港英政府想要的，究竟是民主還是變相的殖民地自決？

至於回歸後冒起的諸如「香港城邦論」「香港民族論」「本土自決」等「港獨」思潮，以及對港英統治的「戀殖情結」，於情不符，於法無據，不過是痴人說夢罷了。

為什麼中央對香港
有全面管治權？

　　2014 年 6 月國務院新聞辦發表《「一國兩制」在香港
特別行政區的實踐》白皮書，提及中央擁有對香港特區
的全面管治權。香港有人對此大加撻伐，稱「全面管治」
就是「什麼都管」「一國一制」，是對基本法的「僭建」。
這些無端的指責，暴露出在中央與特區關係上巨大的
盲區。

　　「全面管治權」並不費解。首先它是國家主權的固有
權力，從香港回歸起就存在。其次它與特區高度自治權
並行不悖，絕非什麼都管。

　　為什麼是固有權力？辛亥革命以後的歷屆中國政府
始終沒有放棄對香港的主權，只是因為被英國強佔而無
法管治香港，從而無法行使主權。中國政府收回香港，
恢復行使主權，也就收回了治權。習近平主席說得明
白：「香港從回歸之日起，重新納入國家治理體系。」全
面管治權是主權的體現，收回卻不能管治，收回就失去

了意義。

為什麼説並行不悖？在「一國兩制」下，特區自治範圍內的地方事務由特區政府負責，實行高度自治。高度自治是全面管治權在特別行政區的特殊實現方式，或者説，高度自治權是全面管治權的有機組成部分，全面管治權在很大程度上通過高度自治權來實現。

主權即最終決定權，是一個國家對其領土內的一切人和物享有的排他性管轄權。中國是單一制國家，不獨香港，中央對所有地方行政區域都擁有全面管治權。主權只有一個，只能屬於國家，而不能與地方分享。主權與治權也不能分割，主權是治權的依據，是治權合法性的來源；治權是主權的行使方式，喪失治權，主權就成了空中樓閣。中央依據主權決定對香港的管治方式，包括選擇有利於保障中央行使主權、落實全面管治權的政治體制，這是確立行政主導體制的重要考慮。

當年戴卓爾夫人訪華及後來的中英談判中，英方先是主張「條約有效論」，試圖憑藉不平等條約繼續侵佔香港主權，被鄧小平以「主權問題不是一個可以討論的問題」懟回；繼而提出「主權換治權」，即承認中國對香港擁有主權，但繼續由英國人管治，這同樣遭到中方堅決拒絕，鄧小平說「香港人是能治理好香港的」。

有人說「一國兩制」是主權歸中央，治權歸香港。這與「主權換治權」是同樣的邏輯，是對主權的割裂。設立特別行政區，實行「一國兩制」，並未改變中國一個主權、一部憲法、一個中央的單一制國家形式。香港的高度自治權並非與生俱來，沒有主權下的全面管治，就沒有授權下的高度自治。同時，中央充分尊重和堅定維護特區享有的高度自治權。

白皮書寫明，全面管治權既包括中央直接行使的權力，也包括授權特區高度自治；對特區的高度自治權，中央具有監督權。中央權力中央行使，特區權力在中央監督下行使，依法行權，取予有道，既不放棄責任，亦不越俎代庖，中央就是這麼做的。

為什麼中央全面管治權與特區高度自治權相統一？

　　中央全面管治權與特區高度自治權相統一，基於國家治理和特區治理的必然邏輯，是特區制度設計的內在要求，是「一國兩制」有效運作的重要保證。

　　特區享有行政管理權、立法權、獨立的司法權和終審權，由基本法加以規定，構成特區高度自治權。而在基本法之上，憲法賦予中央實行和規範「一國兩制」的權力，基本法也對中央管理的事務以及中央和特區關係做了規定，由此構成中央對特區的全面管治權。特區以憲法和基本法為基礎的憲制秩序，決定了中央全面管治權與特區高度自治權在憲制上是統一的，兩者緊密銜接才能把特區治理好。

　　中央全面管治權最大的體現，是憲法第 31 條、第 62 條規定，由全國人大決定特別行政區的設立及其制度。憲法和基本法規定的中央對特區直接行使的管治權力還有：全國人大對基本法的修改權；全國人大常委會對基本法的解釋權，對行政長官和立法會產生辦法修改的決定權，對立法會制定的法律備案或發回的監督權，對特區進入緊急狀態的決定權，以及向特區做出新的授權；國務院對行政長官和主要官員的任命權，對與特區有關的外交事務的管理權，以及向行政長官發出指令；中央軍事委員會領導香港駐軍，履行防務職責，等等。舉例來說，2006 年全國人大常委會授權香港對深圳灣港方口岸區依照特區法律實施管轄，就是新的授權。

高度自治權不是完全自治，也不是分權，而是中央授予的地方事務管理權。高度自治權的限度在於中央授予多少權力，特區就享有多少權力，不存在「剩餘權力」，授權以外的權力仍然保留在中央，授權也不限制和約束中央權力。全面管治權是主權性權力，是高度自治權的源頭；高度自治權必須維護全面管治權，而不能排斥和對立。基本法的一些規定，既是對高度自治的保障，也是對特區執行基本法的監督。比如，特區立法會制定的法律須報全國人大常委會備案，這是特區立法的必經程式，如被發回則立即失效。再如，基本法的解釋權屬於全國人大常委會，人大常委會又授權特區法院在審理案件時可對基本法條款進行解釋，但做了具體限定。

　　香港回歸後重新納入國家治理體系，中央全面管治權與特區高度自治權相統一，確保了以國家根本利益和香港整體利益、長遠利益為依歸。把中央依法行使權力說成是對特區高度自治的干預，顯然是錯誤的。鄧小平說，「中央確實是不干預特別行政區的具體事務的」，但是，如果特區發生危害國家和香港根本利益的事情，「那就非干預不行」，「如果中央把什麼權力都放棄了，就可能會出現一些混亂，損害香港的利益。所以，保持中央的某些權力，對香港有利無害」。制定香港國安法，完善特區選舉制度，印證了鄧小平的預見：「總有一些事情沒有中央出頭你們（指香港）是難以解決的。」

為什麼是「行政主導」？

　　香港的治理模式與內地不同，但畢竟是國家治理體系的一部分，其政治體制必須與國家政治體制相適應相銜接。為此，基本法規定了符合特區實際的行政主導體制。

　　鄧小平説：「香港的穩定，除了經濟的發展以外，還要有個穩定的政治制度。」「我們一定要切合實際，要根據自己的特點來決定自己的制度和管理方式。」基本法起草過程中，政治體制設計最費周章。從中央角度考慮，中央管治要有可靠的着力點，否則中央權力就會被架空，高度自治就成了變相的完全自治，由行政長官負責的行政機關是最適合的着力點。從香港角度考慮，要保持繁榮穩定，就要把以往行之有效的元素保留下來，而回歸前香港賴以成功的元素中，行政主導是重要的一條，可以經過改造後沿用。

　　按照基本法的設計，中央對特區行政、立法、司法三權的管轄方式與尺度是有差異的。司法是獨立的，立法會是本地選舉產生的，只有行政長官在本地選舉或協商產生後還須經中央政府任命，特區政府主要官員由行政長官提名後也須報中央政府任命，行政長官還須執行中央政府發出的指令。行政長官既是特區的首長，代表特區，也是特區政府的首長，負責行政事務；既要對特區負責，也要對中央政府負責，要向中央述職。這個「雙首長雙負責」的定位，在特區建制內是獨一無二的，凸顯了行政長官的權威地位和行政權的主導地位，也由此有了「特首」這個簡明而貼切的稱謂。

不難看出，香港特區與中央政府最直接的紐帶就是行政。中央管治香港的法律依據是基本法，主要依託是行政長官和其領導的特區政府，以致有一種說法，中央管香港，一靠基本法，二靠行政長官。有參與特區政制設計的學者，把香港的政治體制直接稱為「行政長官負責制」。行政主導之於香港、之於「一國兩制」的重要意義和作用就在於此。

總之，香港實行以行政長官為核心的行政主導體制，是由我國單一制國家結構和特區直轄於中央政府的地方行政區域的憲制地位決定的，是行政長官對中央負責的有效方式。

　　基本法沒寫「行政主導」四個字，但「政治體制」部分以行政長官、行政機關、立法機關、司法機關、區域組織、公務人員的順序排列，突出了行政權。這與許多國家和地區的憲制性法律中立法在前、行政在後的排序不同，明確無誤體現了行政主導的立法原意。基本法第64條有特區政府對立法會負責的規定，這指的是冒號後面列出的四個具體範疇，並不是指特區政府對立法會有隸屬關係。

　　基本法實施十周年和二十周年的時候，兩任全國人大委員長吳邦國和張德江都提及行政主導，稱這一特殊的設計，符合特區的法律地位，適應香港作為國際性工商業大都會對於政府效能的實際需要，保留了香港原有政制中行之有效的部分，「是最有利於香港發展的制度安排」。習近平主席也強調特區必須堅持實行行政主導體制。

為什麼不是「三權分立」?

　　香港回歸前由《英皇制誥》《皇室訓令》規定的政治體制，回歸後由基本法確立的政治體制，都不是三權分立，而是行政主導。所不同的是，回歸前是集權式的行政主導，回歸後是行政主導，行政與立法相互制衡又相互配合。

　　英國在本土實行議會至上體制，但在其殖民統治地方均實行集權或獨裁的統治方式。在香港，英皇任命港督，港督提名並經英國外交及聯邦事務部同意委任高級官員和行政、立法兩局議員，港督兼任立法局主席，集行政、立法大權於一身。在港英統治一百五十多年的時間裏，經歷了一個由行政獨裁到行政集權，再到有限度開放選舉下行政主導的過程。

　　末代港督彭定康大搞激進政改，美其名曰「加快民主步伐」，實為強立法弱行政，給回歸後的政府管治製造麻煩。時任國務院副總理兼外交部長錢其琛一針見血指出，彭定康意圖對現行香港行政體制做重大改變，變行政主導為立法主導。

現代社會都有行政、立法、司法三種公權力，不過三權關係不盡相同。香港雖有三權分立之形，但行政權明顯居於更權威更主動的地位。特區政府有立法創議權，政府議案優先列入立法會議程，簡單多數通過，議員議案的通過則有更高的門檻。基本法第74條規定，立法會議員不能提出涉及公共開支、政治體制及政府運作的法案；如果提出涉及政府政策的法案，必須事前得到行政長官書面同意，可惜這一條沒有很好執行。行政對司法的制約則包括行政長官依照法定程序任免各級法院法官，有權赦免或減刑，行政長官就國家行為的事實問題所發出的證明文件對法院有約束力等。

政府的有效管治是社會穩定與發展的保障，政治體制要確保政府實施有效管治。1990年3月全國人大審議基本法時，起草委員會做出說明：「行政機關和立法機關之間的關係應該是既相互制衡又相互配合；為了保持香港穩定和行政效率，行政長官應有實權，但同時也要受到制約。」有別於港英行政主導的集權色彩，基本法確立行政主導、司法獨立、行政與立法相互制衡又相互配

合的政治體制，目的是建立一個在民主參與和民主監督
基礎上的高效政府，有香港學者稱之為「行政主導下的
三權分立」。

　　鄧小平明確指出，「香港的制度也不能完全西化，
不能照搬西方的一套」，「如果完全照搬，比如搞三權分
立，搞英美的議會制度，並以此來判斷是否民主，恐怕
不適宜」。行政主導與立法主導、三權分立是不同的管治
模式。美國是三權分立，三權之間分庭抗禮，憲法中的
排序是國會在前，總統和司法在後。英國是立法主導，
實行議會內閣制，由議會多數黨掌握行政權力。因為立
法系統與司法系統沒有上下級隸屬關係，所以立法主
導、三權分立適合於國家層面，而不適合單一制國家受
中央管轄的地方。昔日是英國的「海外屬土」，現在是中
國的地方行政區，這就決定了香港只能行政主導，不能
三權分立。

為什麼必須堅持「愛國者治港」?

「港人治港」是「一國兩制」的重要特徵,回歸後中央政府沒有向特區政府派一官一吏。但「港人治港」與高度自治一樣,都有特定的內涵和邊界。高度自治不是完全自治,「港人治港」必須是愛國者治港。

鄧小平講,「港人治港有個界線和標準,就是必須由愛國者為主體的港人來治理香港」,未來特區政府的管理,「參與者的條件只有一個,就是愛國者」。什麼人是「愛國者」? 鄧小平給出的標準是,「尊重自己民族,誠心誠意擁護祖國恢復行使對香港的主權,不損害香港的繁榮和穩定」。講這段話的時間是 1984 年,也就是說,在「一國兩制」最初的設計中,愛國者治港就是硬要求。基本法第 104 條規定,主要官員、立法會議員、法院法官等公務人員,在就職時必須依法宣誓擁護《中華人民共和國香港特別行政區基本法》,效忠中華人民共和國香港特別行政區,這是愛國者治港的一個具體體現。

　　「愛國者管治」是國際通則，沒有哪個國家或地方會把管治權交給不忠於自己國家的人。各國對公務人員均有政治效忠的要求。英國法律規定「賣國者」不得參加議會選舉。美國參眾兩院均設有道德委員會，監督議員是否有不忠於聯邦的行為。特區政權機構是國家機構的一部分，愛國是特區公務人員基本的政治倫理。中央絕對不會允許不愛國乃至與中央對抗的人掌握特區管治權。掌握重要權力、肩負重要管治責任的人，必須是堅定的愛國者。

　　以往有反中亂港分子包括「港獨」分子通過選舉進入立法會等特區管治架構，阻撓政府施政，抗拒中央管治，損害市民福祉。他們公然提出「攬炒」策略並設計了具體步驟，企圖奪取立法會和選委會過半議席，最終奪取特區最高權力。這種狀況暴露出特區選舉制度的漏洞。選舉是進入管治架構的重要途徑，必須從制度上確保愛國者上位、亂港者出局。2021 年全國人大修改完善了香港特區選舉制度，就是用法律確保愛國者治港落到實處，並最終形成符合香港實際的民主選舉制度。

　　完善後的選制健全了資格審查，防止不愛國的人進入管治架構。此外，新選制調整功能界別組成，更好地體現均衡參與；由同一個選委會產生行政長官候選人和部分立法會議員，選民基礎有共同點，有利於行政與立法的溝通和行政主導。新選制不排斥持反政府意見的人，只要符合愛國者標準，都有機會參選。

2021 年 1 月 27 日，習近平主席聽取林鄭月娥行政長官述職時指出：「香港由亂及治的重大轉折，再次昭示了一個深刻道理，那就是要確保『一國兩制』實踐行穩致遠，必須始終堅持『愛國者治港』。這是事關國家主權、安全、發展利益，事關香港長期繁榮穩定的根本原則。」為什麼是根本原則？因為處理好「一國」與「兩制」的關係，落實中央全面管治權，維護憲法和基本法確立的憲制秩序，所有這些「一國兩制」的基本要求，都有賴於愛國者治港，否則就無從談起。

為什麼《中英聯合聲明》 不是基本法的效力來源？

　　基本法晚於《中英聯合聲明》，並拓展了《聯合聲明》中中方十二條對港方針政策，因此有觀點說，基本法的效力源自《聯合聲明》，英方有權依據《聯合聲明》監督香港「一國兩制」的執行情況。這個說法對嗎？

　　請留意，《聯合聲明》條文中，有些是中國政府聲明，有些是英國政府聲明，有些則是兩國政府聲明。採取這種形式，是因為有些內容雙方意見一致而共同表述，有些不一致則分別表述，最終求同存異形成「聯合」聲明。對九七回歸的表述，中方是「對香港恢復行使主權」，英方是「將香港交還給中華人民共和國」，字面沒有明顯歧義，又顧及各自立場，不失為一種巧妙的處理。《聯合聲明》包含三項內容，一是明確香港回歸，二是回歸後中國政府對港方針政策，三是回歸前過渡期的安排。英國政府的權利和義務在一、三兩項，這兩項已經履行完畢。第二項是中國政府自己的聲明，已納入基本法，由中國政府在香港實施，與英國沒有權利義務關係。中方在中英談判時就強調，中國政府對港方針政策純屬中國內政，無需另一國批准或監督。中國外交部一再申明，九七後香港事務是中國內政，英國無主權，無治權，也無監督權。

《聯合聲明》不是基本法的效力來源，也不是基本法的法律基礎，基本法的法律基礎是中國憲法。憲法第 31 條是特區設立和特區制度立法的依據。基本法序言寫明，它是根據憲法制定的。憲法是基本法的母法，沒有憲法就不會有基本法。中國政府將「十二條」寫入《聯合聲明》，是「一國兩制」方針政策的梳理和宣示，而不是為基本法立法授權。早在 1981 年，全國人大葉劍英委員長代表中國政府提出和平統一台灣的九條方針政策（簡稱「葉九條」），就勾勒了「一國兩制」的基本意涵。

憲法是主權的最高體現。中國只有一部憲法，基本法是特區的憲制性法律，把它稱為「香港的小憲法」只是一種比喻。香港不僅要遵從基本法，也要遵從憲法。這並不是說憲法的所有條款都直接適用於香港，而是說香港作為一個地方行政區，必須尊重和維護憲法規定的國家制度和體制。同時，憲法中屬「一國」主權範疇的內容，則對香港直接適用。比如，台灣是中國的一部分，完成統一祖國大業是全中國人民的神聖職責，香港當然必須遵守，不能例外。

基本法將「一國兩制」由方針構想變為法律制度，是一個艱巨的再創造過程。內地和香港人士共同組成起草委員會，兩次公開向社會徵求意見，逐條推敲打磨，耗時四年八個月。如果從「一國兩制」構想提出算起，堪稱十年磨一劍。鄧小平稱讚這是「一部具有歷史意義和國際意義的法律」，「一個具有創造性的傑作」。基本法於香港回歸之日起實施，卻提早七年頒佈，讓香港居民看到「一國兩制」未來的樣貌，穩定了人心，成為「一國兩制」不可或缺的法律保障。

為什麼說「一國兩制」是「大變」？

「馬照跑、股照炒」，這是當年對回歸後的香港通俗而生動的描述。的確，許多人對「一國兩制」的理解就是「什麼都不變」。不過，這個理解太表像化了，鄧小平說，「『一國兩制』就是大變」。事實上，自回歸那天起，香港就在演奏着變與不變的交響曲。

沒錯，基本法寫的是五十年不變，香港還是自由港和獨立關稅區，使用的還是港幣，英語仍與中文一樣是官方語言，這些具有香港特色的林林總總，都保留下來了。

但是，換個角度就會發現，香港有了根本性的改變，那就是憲制基礎變了。港英統治下的香港，憲制性法律是《英皇制誥》《皇室訓令》，依此確立殖民統治。香港是英國的「海外屬土」，公務人員效忠的是英皇。回歸後，憲法和基本法共同構成特區的憲制基礎，公務人員要宣誓擁護基本法，效忠特區。有了這個新的憲制基礎，就構建起一套與之相適應的制度和體制，香港原有的特色和優勢得以保存下來。換句話說，有了憲制基礎這個最大的變，就有了香港其他方面的穩定和不變。

法治是社會的立身之本。香港回歸後原有的資本主義制度和生活方式不變，法律基本不變。為什麼法律不是「不變」而是「基本不變」？不僅因為有了基本法，還因為原有法律都需要依基本法來重新檢視。回歸前，根據基本法第 160 條，全國人大常委會歷時五年對香港原有法律進行了審查，把那些與基本法抵觸的甄別出來，確認大部分原有法律不抵觸基本法，可以採用為特別行政區的法律。當然，這些法律中諸如「女皇陛下」「王室」之類的表述，要根據回歸後的中央與特區關係做「適應化」的替換。

憲法是特區制度的法律淵源，基本法根據憲法第 31 條制定，將「一國兩制」方針法律化、制度化。在香港的法律中，基本法具有凌駕地位，規定了中央和特區關係、特區政權的組成和功能、特區居民的權利和義務，與港英憲制已是天壤之別。

鄧小平說：「不要籠統地說怕變。如果有什麼要變，一定是變得更好，更有利於香港的繁榮和發展，而不會損害香港人的利益。」回歸後的香港，在不變中感受着變。以前港英高官看着倫敦來的電報辦事，而今特區政府自己決策。以前的港督是英皇派來的，而今的行政長官是港人組成的選舉委員會選出來，再由中央政府任命的。以前的立法局議員大都由港督委任，港督自己兼任立法局主席，而今的立法會議員是選出來的，主席由議員互選產生。以前的終審權在倫敦的樞密院，而今特區設立了終審法院，有獨立的司法權和終審權。香港各項選舉的民主成分不斷擴大，港區全國人大代表和政協委員直接在國家層面參政議政。

憲制基礎改變的一個重要標誌，是香港重新納入國家治理體系。特區需要適應新的憲制，完善同憲法和基本法實施相關的制度和機制。加強香港社會特別是對公務人員和青少年的憲法和基本法宣傳教育，殊為重要。

為什麼「一國兩制」可以長期堅持？

香港回歸祖國二十五周年，習近平主席向全世界鄭重宣示，「一國兩制」是經過實踐檢驗了的「好制度」，「沒有任何理由改變，必須長期堅持！」這無疑是對鄧小平所講「五十年不變，五十年以後也不變」的再次承諾。「一國兩制」長期不變、長期堅持，依據是什麼呢？

要回答這個問題，先要看看鄧小平講五十年不變的前提是什麼？這個前提是否發生了改變？

當年鄧小平講五十年不變有兩個前提。一個前提是「兩個不變」。他是這樣講的：「說不變不是一個方面不變，而是兩個方面不變。……要真正能做到五十年不變，五十年以後也不變，就要大陸這個社會主義制度不變。」這就是說，內地不變，香港才會不變。再一個前提是實現「三步走」目標。他提出的「三步走」戰略目標是到本世紀中葉我國達到中等發達國家水平，這恰好是五十年不變的節點。那時，國家的主體強大了，局部地區就會更加穩定，這樣一來誰還想變呢？鄧小平沒有想到的是，改革開放令中國創造了經濟發展的奇跡，他規劃的「三步走」大大提前了。中共十九大重新調整了戰略發展目標，到本世紀中葉要建成社會主義現代化強國。

時至今日，五十年不變的兩個前提不僅沒有改變，而且更加堅實。從鄧小平到習近平，兩代中共領導人對「一國兩制」充滿信心，說到底是對中國特色社會主義充滿信心，對中華民族偉大復興充滿信心。鄧小平講不變是一種預見，習近平講不變則有了堅實的實踐依據。「一國兩制」經過實踐洗禮，具備自我調適和糾偏的能力，證明是一種有效的治理模式。從中央來說，已經把「一國兩制」列為國家治理的顯著優勢和基本方略，毫無疑問將長期堅持，不會變、不動搖。

當然，「一國兩制」能否長期堅持不能只看中央，還要看香港，畢竟香港是「一國兩制」實踐的主體。前些年香港「黑暴」「港獨」猖獗，令許多人憂心忡忡：中央能容忍這樣的高度自治嗎？2047 年以後還有「一國兩制」嗎？這不是杞人憂天，的確有一些香港內外的破壞勢力總想讓「一國兩制」脫軌、變質，對此必須始終保持警惕。只要「一國兩制」實踐不走樣、不變形，就不必擔憂

2047 乃至更久的未來。

　　現在談 2047 為時尚早，但有一點可以成為思考「變與不變」的參照。按照基本法序言，當年確定實行「一國兩制」且五十年不變，考慮了「香港的歷史和現實情況」。五十年後變不變，肯定也要看那時的歷史和現實情況。到了 2047，如果基本法有效貫徹，「兩制」相得益彰，國家和香港都繁榮穩定，「一國兩制」當然就會延續。

　　「五十年不變」寫入了基本法，有法律的嚴肅性，但不妨把它理解為「長期不變」的另一種表達。鄧小平說：「五十年只是一個形象的說法，五十年後也不會變。前五十年是不能變，五十年之後是不需要變。」期待他的預言成真。

為什麼說回歸後香港開啟真正的民主？

　　回歸後香港居民享有的政治參與權是港英時代無法比擬的。有人指責中央拖慢了香港民主發展的步伐，這是罔顧事實，既缺乏歷史比較，也缺乏對基本法相關原則的認知。

　　2021年11月，國務院新聞辦發表《「一國兩制」下香港的民主發展》白皮書。這份繼2014年後又一關於香港的白皮書，以詳盡的事實，描述了香港回歸前後的民主狀況和中央堅定支持香港民主發展的努力，進一步闡明了中央對香港民主發展的原則立場，是重要的正本清源。

　　香港的殖民制度被稱作「早期帝國政治的活化石」。從英國佔領香港一直到上世紀六十年代前，政治權力始終掌握在港督及英籍官員手中，佔香港人口98%的華人難以參政，僅有個別人士被「吸納」進行政、立法兩局，點綴「政治開明」。1976年英國政府批准《公民權利與政治權利國際公約》時，明確排除《公約》關於定期選舉的規定在香港實施。港英政府一位英籍高官 1981 年退休後發表演講，坦言他任職官員的三十年間，「民主」一直是「骯髒的字眼」，港英官員堅信，引入民主政治將是摧毀香港經濟、製造社會和政治不穩的最快、最有效的辦法。1982 年香港首次選舉部分區議會議員，港英政府自詡是「香港推行市民參與政治初期中成功的第一步」，這時中國將收回香港早已世人皆知。1991 年首次有部分立法局議員由分區直選產生，這時基本法已經頒佈了。

前英國首相戴卓爾夫人在其回憶錄中披露，早在中英談判時，發現由英國繼續管治香港已不可能，於是就「必須發展香港的民主架構，以期在短期內完成獨立或自治的目標」。港英政府從 1980 年代開始拋出一連串代議政治白皮書，全面佈局，急速開放選舉，直至彭定康搞激進政改，都貫穿着這個預謀。在香港擴大民主選舉問題上，英國人是算計過的，如果他們繼續管治香港，激進政改根本就不會發生。而激進政改形成的「路徑依賴」，有違基本法確立的原則，給回歸後特區民主發展埋下禍根。

香港回歸後建立了制度層面的民主，開啟了民主的新紀元。「港人治港」是最大的民主，徹底結束了回歸前英國人全面掌控香港行政、立法和司法終審權的局面。特區政府和立法會均由本地人組成，行政長官選舉委員會人數和立法會直選議席逐屆增加。如果不是反對派的阻撓，2017 年和 2020 年，香港就可以實現「雙普選」了。

不能拋開社會條件孤立地處理選舉問題。基本法第 45 條和第 68 條都明確界定，行政長官和立法會的產生辦法要「根據香港特別行政區的實際情況和循序漸進的原則而規定」。問題不在是否普選，而在於急進還是漸進，是從抽象的概念出發還是根據香港的實際情況來安排。從有直選到實現普選，法國用了一百四十年，美國用了一百七十年，英國用了五百六十年。脫離社會承受能力急於實行普選，只會帶來社會的分化和動盪，過猶不及，最終可能付出拖垮經濟和法治的沉重代價。

為什麼「雙普選」被卡住了？

2015 年 6 月 18 日，立法會的反對派議員否決了特區政府根據全國人大常委會「8 · 31」決定提出的 2017 年行政長官普選方案，已經打開的「雙普選」大門，被他們關上了。

這已經不是第一次 —— 2005 年也有一份擴大選舉民主成分的政改方案被「民主派」議員捆綁否決，憤怒的市民從此給他們改名叫「反對派」。

《中英聯合聲明》沒講普選，是基本法確定了「雙普選」的目標，中國政府是特區民主制度的設計者和堅定推進者。基本法第 45 條規定，行政長官「最終達至由一個有廣泛代表性的提名委員會按民主程序提名後普選產生的目標」；第 68 條規定，立法會「最終達至全部議員由普選產生的目標」。2007 年 12 月 29 日，全國人大常委會作出決定，給出了「雙普選」的時間表，即 2017 年可以普選行政長官，隨後可以普選立法會。2014 年的

「8‧31」決定承接「12‧29」決定，對行政長官普選辦法的一些核心問題作出規定。如果沒有開頭那一幕，「雙普選」已經落袋了。

反對派否決政改方案的理由是「8‧31」決定有「篩選」，因而不是「真普選」，要求中央收回。他們指責的「篩選」有兩點：一個是「提名權」，他們主張增加政黨提名和公民提名，但這變相架空了提名委員會，違反了基本法；另一個是「過半數」，他們不肯接受「每名候選人均須獲得全體委員半數以上支持」的規定，要求「降低門檻」。誰都知道，少數服從多數是民主的通行規則，反對派連這個也反對，說穿了就是擔心推不出他們自己的候選人。

篩選合理嗎？解釋這個問題，要回到「一國」與「兩制」關係和「愛國者治港」的原則上來。基本法規定由提名委員會作為整體「機構提名」，「8‧31」決定將基本法要求的「按民主程序提名」確定為「半數以上」，目的是要依靠多數人的理性，防止選出與中央對抗，最終傷及國家主權安全，也會給香港帶來危害的行政長官候選人。「港人治港」是愛國者治港，行政長官是「港人治港」的最高代表，必須由堅定的愛國者擔任，「8‧31」決定強調「這是『一國兩制』方針政策的基本要求」，「行政長官普選辦法必須為此提供相應的制度保證」。

提名就是篩選，這一點毋庸諱言。美國由兩大黨提名總統候選人，英國由執政黨提名首相，都是篩選。行政長官在「一國兩制」中的角色太重要了，既對特區負責，也對中央負責；既要港人擁護，亦要中央信任，惟其如此，參選人必須先過提名關，普選產生後還要經中央政府任命。明白了這一點，就會明白，「8・31」決定退無可退。

《「一國兩制」下香港的民主發展》白皮書說，「二十多年來香港民主發展過程中出現的主要問題，實質不是要不要民主的問題，而是要不要維護『一國』原則的問題」，可謂一針見血。

為什麼要構建有香港特色的民主選舉制度？

香港所謂的「民主派」急於實現「雙普選」，把香港所有問題的根源歸結為沒有「一人一票」。他們主張的選舉制度，與香港在「一國兩制」下應有的選舉制度大相徑庭。

對特區的選舉制度，鄧小平講過明確的意見。他說：「對香港來說，普選就一定有利？我不相信。」「這些管理香港事務的人應該是愛祖國、愛香港的香港人，普選就一定能選出這樣的人來嗎？」「即使搞普選，也要有一個逐步的過渡，要一步一步來。」「如果硬要照搬（西方的一套），造成動亂，那是很不利的。」

選舉制度沒有國際標準，美國與英國的選舉制度就不一樣。有人依據《公民權力與政治權利國際公約》第25條，稱「普及而平等」就是民主選舉的國際標準，他們冠冕堂皇的口號很容易矇騙人。實際上，25條只明確了選舉的若干原則，並沒有規定具體方式。1994年聯合國出版《人權與選舉：選舉的法律、技術和人權手冊》，指出「沒有一套政治制度或選舉方法適合所有人和所有國家」，並明確反對「將任何一個已有的政治模式強加於任何地方」。

評判選舉制度的優劣，最重要的標準要看它是否適合該國或該地區的實際情況。鞋子合不合腳，穿了才知道。衡量香港選舉制度的標準不是西方國家的既有模式，而是兩個特定條件。首先是憲制地位。作為單一制國家的地方行政區域，香港的選舉是一國之內的地方性選舉，不能照搬主權國家的選舉制度，必須從國家利益與安全、從中央和特區關係的角度去考慮和設計。其次是實際情況。要循序漸進，讓民主進程與社會及歷史條件相適應，依法有序發展，防止急進震盪和極端民主。要均衡參與，兼顧各階層各界別，以利於經濟發展和社會穩定。要有助於處理行政與立法關係，落實基本法確立的行政主導體制，實現良政善治。

順帶說一句，「循序漸進」最早是港督衞奕信提出的，得到鄧小平的贊同，寫進了基本法。

世界上不存在放之四海皆準的民主標準和模式。民主是豐富多樣的，不能等同於選舉，更不能等同於直選。擴大協商、諮詢等多種民主形式，追求優質民主和從選舉到治理的全過程民主，才能更好體現社會整體利益和共同意願。政制發展是為了帶來良政善治，並非「一人一票」那麼簡單。西方政府陷入「選舉遊戲」和「否決政治」的怪圈，正在變得失效，很值得港人深思。

基本法明確了普選目標，更明確了香港的憲制地位和實現普選的條件。不能談選舉目標就搬出基本法，談選舉辦法就拋開基本法。2021年修訂完善的特區選舉制度，是對原有制度的重構及優化，與現階段香港民主發展的需要相契合。未來香港走向普選，那也將是符合「一國兩制」、有香港特色的普選。歸根結底，必須在憲法和基本法的軌道上推動香港民主的發展。

為什麼中央出手制定
香港國安法？

　　2020 年 6 月 30 日，全國人大常委會通過了《中華人民共和國香港特別行政區維護國家安全法》，結束了國家安全在香港不設防的歷史。為什麼基本法 23 條已經授權特區就維護國家安全立法，還要由全國人大常委會直接制定香港國安法呢？

　　香港國安法是一部遲到的法律。國家安全是國家主權的要義，本應由中央統一立法和執法。鑒於內地與香港法律制度的差異，中央以基本法 23 條授權特區立法，這是「一國兩制」下的特殊安排，是對特區的高度信任。可惜，23 條遲遲未能立法，以致前些年香港「港獨」「黑暴」「攬炒」橫行，反中亂港勢力挾洋自重，「修例風波」演化成港版「顏色革命」，製造了回歸後最大的動亂，嚴重威脅國家安全和特區政權安全，已經到了鄧小平所警示的「非中央出手不行」的地步。中央對國家安全負有根本責任，可以行使一切必要的權力，這種責任和權力並不因為 23 條向特區授權而喪失。在特區層面難有作為的情況下，中央必須果斷出手，從國家層面推進國安立法。

安全是發展的保障。香港國安法的目的只有一個，就是維護國家安全和特區政權安全。香港國安法防範、制止和懲治的分裂國家、顛覆國家政權、恐怖活動、勾結外國或者境外勢力危害國家安全罪，都是香港前些年尤其是「修例風波」中為害最烈的危害國家安全的行為。香港國安法只針對極少數犯罪分子，同時保護基本法規定的言論自由等合法權益。

針對香港維護國家安全既存在法律漏洞，又缺乏執行機制的缺陷，香港國安法既規定了必須懲治的四類罪行，也規定了必備的執行機制，以確保法律落地。包括設立特區維護國家安全委員會、中央指派國安事務顧問、警務處設立國安部門、律政司設立國安案件檢控部門、行政長官指定審理國安案件法官，以及就特區國安事務向中央提交報告等。還有一個重要的機制建設，就是設立中央政府駐港維護國家安全公署，監督、指導、協調、支持特區履行維護國家安全的職責。如果出現香港國安法第 55 條的三種特殊情況，則出駐港國安公署及內地司法機關直接管轄案件，並適用內地法律。設立特區層面與中央層面兩套執法機制，是「一國兩制」實踐的重大創新。

香港國安法並不取代 23 條，也未完全涵蓋 23 條所列七種犯罪行為。香港國安法第 7 條明確，特區應當盡早完成 23 條立法。內地適用的《中華人民共和國國家安全法》不在香港實施，而是量身定制香港國安法；特區對絕大多數國安案件行使管轄權，獨立檢控和審判，以及香港國安法不取代 23 條立法，這些都是堅持「一國兩制」、充分考慮香港實際情況的體現。

「一國」是「兩制」的載體，沒有國家安全的「一國兩制」是靠不住的。習近平主席劃出了「一國兩制」必須堅守的「三條底線」，香港國安法是三條底線的法制化。

為什麼 23 條立法
不能再拖了？

　　香港回歸祖國已經二十多年，有一項必須履行的憲制責任拖延至今，這就是基本法 23 條立法。在香港國安法頒佈之前，由於 23 條未能立法的缺陷，香港成為國家安全的一塊短板。

　　中央給予香港「一國兩制」特殊地位，是以實現和維護國家統一為前提的。23 條規定特區應自行立法禁止危害國家安全的七種行為，與其說是授權立法，不如說是責成立法。2015 年頒佈的《中華人民共和國國家安全法》明確要求，港澳兩個特別行政區「應當履行維護國家安全的責任」。「皮之不存，毛將焉附」。在國安問題上，只有「一國」之責，沒有「兩制」之分；「一國」都保護不了，何談「兩制」！

　　有人主張先立 23 條再搞「雙普選」，此話不無道理。國安立法開天窗，普選的政治風險顯而易見。但中央沒有把兩者硬性掛鈎，全國人大在 2007 年就給出了

「雙普選」的時間表，這是中央充分相信港人的又一例證。基本法規定的責任是憲制責任，特區必須履行，而不能選擇性履行。無論是否普選，23 條都要立法。

特區負有維護國家安全的憲制責任和主體責任。2003 年特區政府嘗試 23 條立法未成，此後遲遲未能重啟。香港現有法律中也有一些涉及國安的規定，但這些法律未能完整覆蓋 23 條的範圍，無法替代 23 條立法。況且由於種種原因，這些法律條款長期「沉睡」。前些年反中亂港勢力內外勾聯，嚴重危及國家安全和特區政權安全，突顯了 23 條立法缺失的巨大隱患。國安堪虞是最大的制度漏洞。2019 年 10 月，正是香港「黑暴」猖獗之時，中共十九屆四中全會以中央決定的方式，明確要求「建立健全特別行政區維護國家安全的法律制度和執行機制」。中央出手制定香港國安法，及時彌補了法律空隙，對香港迅速止暴制亂、恢復正常秩序、實現由亂及治的轉折，發揮了關鍵作用。同時也警示特區，23 條立法不能再拖延下去了！

香港國安法與 23 條立法都是特區維護國家安全的重要法律，不能相互取代。23 條立法可以補充香港國安法未規定或未詳細規定的部分，與香港國安法共同築牢國安屏障。

擔心 23 條立法侵蝕人權是多慮了，國安立法針對的是犯罪行為。何況，無論國際公約還是人權法案都寫明，人權與自由不能凌駕國家安全與公共秩序。

當年鄧小平對「不一定在香港駐軍」的說法發了脾氣，強調駐軍是主權的象徵，也是為了防止香港「發生危害國家根本利益的事情」。不能不佩服鄧小平的先見之明，他早就判斷香港會出現「破壞力量」。香港「如果發生動亂，中央政府就要加以干預」，必要時駐軍也會出動。有人擔心出動駐軍就意味着「一國兩制」終結，其實沒那麼嚴重。基本法第 14 條寫明，「香港特別行政區政府在必要時，可向中央人民政府請求駐軍協助維持社會治安和救助災害」。平亂和國防一樣，都是駐軍職責所在。

為什麼中央打出「組合拳」?

2020 年 5 月全國人大做出建立健全香港特區維護國家安全的法律制度和執行機制的決定,據此,人大常委會制定了香港國安法。2021 年 3 月全國人大做出完善香港特區選舉制度的決定,據此,人大常委會修改了基本法附件一和附件二,特區修改了本地有關法律。這兩大舉措是一對「組合拳」,對症下藥,立竿見影。

回歸後香港的亂象可以歸結為兩大問題。一是「穩不住」,反中亂港勢力內外勾結,社會動盪,「港獨」泛起,威脅國家安全和特區穩定。二是「管不好」,深陷「泛政治化」泥潭,立法會「拉布」不止,政府管治效能不彰。這兩大問題在 2019 年「修例風波」中登峰造極,如不盡快解決,最終會拖垮香港,葬送「一國兩制」。鑒於特區政府缺乏足夠的政治能量,解決這兩大問題只能由中央出手,「組合拳」針對的就是這兩大問題。全國人大是國家最高權力機關,回歸前就香港問題做過八次決定，回歸後二十多年只做了上述兩次決定，足見分量之重。

事實證明，香港國安法有效止暴制亂，社會迅速恢復秩序與安寧；修改後的選舉制度堵住了反中亂港分子染指特區管治權的路徑，政府施政趨於順暢。這套「組合拳」讓香港既要穩得住，又要管得好，為解決其他深層次問題創造了條件，進一步夯實了「一國兩制」行穩致遠的制度基礎。

「組合拳」是「一國兩制」初心的堅守。鄧小平提出「一國兩制」是有前提的，最大的前提就是國家的統一以及國家主體的制度不能變，否則「香港的繁榮穩定也會吹的」。還有一個前提是「愛國者治港」，否則「港人治港」就會變質。制定國安法和完善選舉制度，重建了特區的政治秩序和政治倫理，守護了「一國兩制」的初心。

「組合拳」是「一國兩制」制度體系的完善。基本法有兩處「留白」沒有做最終處理。一處是第23條，規定特區應自行立法禁止危害國家安全的七種行為。另一處是選舉辦法，規定最終達致普選，但具體辦法要留待回歸後根據實際情況和循序漸進原則去制定。可惜，23條立法長期擱置，國家安全與特區政權安全受到威脅；選舉辦法不夠完善，令反中亂港勢力搶奪特區管治權有機可乘。制定國安法和完善選舉制度，完成了對基本法的重要補充，堵住了制度漏洞。

「組合拳」也凸顯了依法治港。中央一再強調，要「完善特別行政區同憲法和基本法實施相關的制度和機制」。建立健全法律制度和確保其落實的執行機制，是完善特區治理的治本之策，比其他方式更為有效。

香港社會長期存在兩個認識誤區。一個是國家觀的誤區，擺不正「一國」與「兩制」的關係，甚至置國家利益與安全於不顧。另一個是民主觀的誤區，盲目崇拜西方民主，不考慮香港的實際情況尤其是憲制地位給民主發展框定的邊界。中央打出「組合拳」，明確香港維護國家安全的責任，構建符合香港實際的民主選舉制度，有助於香港社會在認識上撥亂反正。

為什麼「一國兩制」有巨大包容性？

　　資本主義和社會主義曾經在上個世紀分成兩大陣營激烈對抗，制度差異是顯而易見的。在一國之內實行這樣兩種不同的社會制度，並讓它們相得益彰，需要巨大的政治勇氣和包容精神。

　　如此大膽的創意，植根於海納百川、求同存異的中華文化和中國智慧。這不是求大同存小異，而是求大同存大異。由於以和平方式收回香港，喜歡與不喜歡的、同內地適應與不適應的，中央都接受了，寄望在「一國」之內逐漸磨合。鄧小平說，只要維護民族大局，「不管抱什麼政治觀點，包括罵共產黨的人，都要大團結」。習近平概括了「兩個建設好」：「既要把實行社會主義制度的內地建設好，也要把實行資本主義制度的香港建設好。」這就是「一國兩制」寬廣博大的追求。

　　香港的高度自治超過了許多聯邦制國家的州。回歸後，香港保留了自由港和獨立關稅區地位，保留了獨立的財政、稅收、貨幣體系，保留了普通法制度。還有兩點更獨特：一是不向國家繳一分錢稅，也不承擔駐軍費用，當年駐港英軍的軍費是由香港人掏腰包的；二是有獨立的終審權，而回歸前的終審權在倫敦的英國樞密院。終審權是國家主權性權力，各國的地方不享有終審權，以免法制的不統一殃及國家政治的穩定。基本法賦予香港終審權，充分考慮了香港實行普通法制度的實際情況，是對傳統國家治理方式的突破。

中央不僅授權香港高度自治，而且對港人高度信任。港英最後一屆政府二十三名主要官員，除一名外國人按基本法規定不能繼續任職、一人準備退休而被替換外，其餘二十一人均經中央任命進入首屆特區政府，十八萬公務員也悉數留任。中央政府不干預特區內部事務，而且吸納香港同胞加入國家最高權力機關和政治協商機構共商國是，還從香港選拔公務人員代表國家到國際組織去工作。就連事關國家安危、本可由全國人大立法後在香港實施的國家安全法律，也以基本法第 23 條授權特區自行立法。

不妨把中央的對港政策概括成「堵與疏」。堵，就是堅守習近平主席明確的「三條底線」，即絕對不能允許任何危害國家主權安全、挑戰中央權力和基本法權威、利用香港對內地進行滲透破壞的活動，這是「一國」的必然要求。疏，就是鼓勵香港融入國家發展大局，共同推進改革開放和民族復興。CEPA、國家五年規劃、粵港澳大灣區建設、各種在內地生活和就業的便利措施等等，都是香港繁榮發展的新機遇。這一堵一疏，堵是剛性的，疏是號召和期盼，堵與疏之間為香港高度自治提供了巨大空間。

「一國兩制」是一種最大限度平衡國家利益與香港利益的制度設計，用哲學術語來講，這是矛盾統一體。「兩制」之間既有矛盾的一面，又有統一的一面，最大的公約數就是「愛國愛港」。堅持這個共同的核心價值，就能揚長避短，畫出「兩制」最大的同心圓。

結束語：堅定「一國兩制」 制度自信

　　以和平方式恢復行使主權，並在回歸後保持平穩發展，足以證明「一國兩制」是解決歷史遺留問題的最佳方案，也是保持香港長期繁榮穩定的最佳制度安排。平心而論，沒有比「一國兩制」更高明的政治智慧了！

　　「一國兩制」是一項開創性的制度，需要放在歷史與全局的大背景下考察。首先，要把制度與治理區分開。制度提供了社會運行的基本架構，但制度是否有效要靠治理。香港許多問題的根源，在於行政主導受到太多掣肘，社會治理失去效率。其次，要把制度與深層次矛盾區分開。房屋短缺、貧富懸殊等問題回歸前就存在，有些是香港原有制度中固有的矛盾，與「一國兩制」無關。事實恰恰是，因為有了「一國兩制」，香港才能在國家的有力支持下，戰勝金融危機、SARS 等嚴重衝擊，鞏固和保持了國際金融、貿易、航運中心的地位。

　　回過頭看，如果當年特區政府的「八萬五」計劃（每年建造 85,000 套住宅）能夠落實，輪候上樓還會排這麼久嗎？如果少一些內耗，把更多的精力和資源投向經濟民生，香港發展的步伐會不會快一些呢？如果沒有港英「光榮撤退」製造的法律和政治激變，沒有回歸後外部勢力的插手干預，香港會有這麼多亂象嗎？

回歸前，針對香港社會希望保持原有制度及擴大民主的訴求，中央深切體察，以基本法保障五十年不變，並規定了循序漸進的政制發展和普選目標。只要按照基本法去做，這些目標都會實現。遺憾的是，後來出現了脫離基本法軌道爭普選，令香港陷入政治爭拗。前些年泛起的「本土自決」與「港獨」，更是對國家主權的挑戰。這些亂象與「一國兩制」背道而馳，只會與港人的期盼愈走愈遠。

温故而知新。解決香港現實問題的路徑，不是「一國兩制」改弦易轍，不是簡單的「一人一票」，而是按照習近平主席提出的「四點希望」，着力提高治理水平，不斷增強發展動能，切實排解民生憂難，共同維護和諧穩定，讓「一國兩制」的制度優勢更加有效的發揮出來！

當年鄧小平對「一國兩制」充滿信心，今天我們更加充滿信心，習近平主席強調「一國兩制」「沒有任何理由改變，必須長期堅持！」信心來自哪裏？來自「一國兩制」符合國家和香港的整體利益和長遠利益，有巨大的包容性；來自祖國發展日新月異，「兩個一百年」奮鬥目標篤定實現；來自基本法定向指航和中央引領支持，「一國兩制」具備調適能力，能夠解決實踐中遇到的新挑戰新問題。

中華民族偉大復興已經進入不可逆轉的歷史進程，香港「一國兩制」成功實踐是這一歷史進程的重要組成部分。背靠祖國，聯通世界，發揮所長，融合發展，「不為一時之曲折而動搖，不因外部之干擾而迷惘」（習近平語），香港一定能夠續寫「一國兩制」的新篇章。

還是開篇那句話：不忘初心，方得始終。

註： 本書引用的鄧小平先生的講話，均引自三聯書店（香港）有限公司《鄧小平論香港問題》，1993 年 11 月版。

附錄

愛國三問　楊建平

　　幾天前，我受邀參加香港天津聯誼會聚會，慶祝新中國成立七十周年和聯誼會成立二十五周年。會場內歡聲笑語，載歌載舞，滿滿的正能量。

　　我與天津結緣，是因為我的母校南開大學。「文革」後內地恢復高考，我有幸成為首批大學生，在南開度過了美好的四年時光。新中國七十華誕，也恰是南開大學建校百年，剛剛過去的 10 月 17 日，母校舉行了隆重的慶典。

　　沒能返津為母校慶生，頗覺遺憾。這些日子，有關母校的記憶始終縈繞腦海。最最銘記不忘的，當是創校校長張伯苓先生那著名的「愛國三問」。

「你是中國人嗎？」

「你愛中國嗎？」

「你願意中國好嗎？」

　　這振聾發聵的三問，在舊中國苦難深重的年代裏，深深撞擊着掙扎求索的仁人志士的心，激發起一茬又一茬南開人的報國之志、愛國之情，鑄就了南開大學綿延不息的愛國傳統。抗戰時期，日本侵略者轟炸南開校園，試圖摧毀南開人的抗日意志。但南開人是嚇不倒的！一大批南開學子投筆從戎，奔赴抗日前線。張伯苓校長的第三個兒子就是這其中的一員，他加入空軍，搏擊長空，最終捐軀沙場，為祖國付出了年輕的生命。

　　而今，「愛國三問」被大大地鑴寫在南開校園內。新學年開學時，台上，校長一句一句大聲發問，台下，師生們鏗鏘有力報以肯定的回答，此情此景，令人激動不已，熱血沸騰。

　　默誦着「愛國三問」，環顧眼下之香港，我陷入了沉思。

　　習近平主席說：「一個不知道自己來路的民族，是沒有出路的民族。」不少香港青年，不知道近代以來祖國遭受列強欺辱的歷史，不熟悉新中國成立後翻天覆地的深刻變革，也不了解香港與國家榮辱與共、不可分割的緊密聯繫，缺乏對國家和民族的認同感。「滅人之國，必先去其史」，這是英國殖民統治的苦果，也是回歸後香港教育的嚴重缺失。

香港今日之亂，除卻社會民生問題的積怨外，集中暴露了部分港人尤其是青年人對國情認知的偏頗，以至於有人借着「反修例」發泄對國家的仇恨，散播分離和「港獨」理念，竟然可以毫無忌憚、毫不掩飾，足見香港社會國家意識的扭曲已經到了何等嚴重的地步！

痛心之餘，禁不住也生「三問」，想問問香港的青年朋友。

一問，你了解今天的中國嗎？

新中國七十年，由積貧積弱的「東亞病夫」，變成經濟總量超過日本與歐盟之和的世界第二，人均壽命從三十多歲提高到七十多歲。這個十四億人口的大國有着完整的工業體系、卓越的創新能力和強大的國防力量，在國際事務中舉足輕重。改革開放創造了持續四十年的高速增長，平均每三秒鐘就有一個人跨過貧困線，被聯合國歎為奇跡。「北斗」、「蛟龍」、「嫦娥」、「5G」，還有橫跨伶仃洋的港珠澳大橋，驚人的科技發展和基礎建設，令這個國家日新月異。近二十年全球新增森林覆蓋率相當於多出一個亞馬遜雨林，其中四分之一來自中國的貢獻。

你或許不否認中國的經濟成就，但對中國的政治制度嗤之以鼻。的確，如果拿美國式民主做標準，中國恐怕永遠不合格，因為中國不搞多黨制和三權分立。中國也有選舉，但更注重協商，「有事好商量，眾人的事眾人商量」，更能體現民主的真諦。行政、立法、司法、監察，這些現代國家管理的制度模塊中國都有，而政協卻是中國所特有。一黨執政、多黨合作、政治協商，這種政治制度兼顧公平與效率，能夠集中力量辦大事，減少扯皮，更適合中國的國情和快速發展的需要，成為新中國經濟騰飛的制度保障。「經濟很強，政治很糟」，這是西方社會強加於中國的標籤，是一個難以自圓其說的悖論，卻騙了太多的香港人。

二問，你能脫離中國嗎？

香港從來就是中國的領土，回歸後是中國的一個特別行政區。說什麼是香港人而不是中國人，這是荒唐無知加邏輯混亂。你可以離開香港，移民他國，但黑頭髮黃皮膚是與生俱來、無法改變的。無論你是否喜歡，只要你住在香港，你喝的水、用的電、吃的肉類和蔬菜，大部分都來自北方那片大陸。無論你走到哪裏，只要你拿着特區護照，當你在異國他鄉遇到麻煩的時候，能夠幫你的還是中國使館。

一個國家只有一個主權，香港與國家不可分割。那些舉着美國旗、英國旗遊行示威的人，大概是想讓外國政府來保護他們，想讓外國主宰香港。不過現在的中國早已不是近代史上任人宰割的舊中國了，中國政府和十四億國人不會由着這些人喪權辱國的！

三問，你看到中國的未來嗎？

過去七十年，中國人民從站起來到富起來，正在走向強起來。中國的發展藍圖已經繪就，到本世紀中葉將建成富強民主文明和諧美麗的社會主義現代化強國。這也恰恰是香港「一國兩制」五十年不變的節點，「兩制」相得益彰，香港和祖國共享榮光。中國的發展是任何力量都阻擋不了的，經濟總量居世界第一已是指日可待。這不是妄想，制度優勢和經驗積累，以及十四億人的戮力同心，終究會讓中國夢變為現實。

有些人看不到這個前景也不奇怪，時至今日，「歷史終結論」「中國崩潰論」依然不絕於耳。我們已經不挨打了，也已經不挨餓了，但還在挨罵，因為人家控制着話語權和輿論場。中國被西方罵，是因為我們走了一條不

同於西方的國家治理道路。惟其如此，無論中國共產黨
為中國人民也為國際社會辦了多少好事，還要被罵，被
視為另類。中國並不想輸出制度，我們只是找到了一條
適合自己的發展路徑，而且要堅定地走下去。當今世界
正處於百年未有之大變局，其核心是制度的競爭，而中
國真的不懼怕制度競爭！七十年的滄桑巨變給了我們底
氣，令我們對未來充滿自信！

來源：2019 年 10 月 31 日香港《文匯報》
　　　2019 年 11 月 4 日《中國日報香港版》

The Original Intent of "One Country, Two Systems"

An Informal Chat on "One Country, Two Systems"

Preface:
Understanding "one country, two systems" after 25 years of implementation

It has been 25 years since Hong Kong returned to the motherland, as "one country, two systems" has been in practice for just as long and we have definitely learned a lot from so many years of trial and error. President Xi Jinping came to Hong Kong in person to celebrate the 25th anniversary of the Hong Kong Special Administrative Region (HKSAR) and emphasized in his speech at the gathering that the principle of "one country, two systems" must be adhered to for a long time to come, while answering the most important theoretical and realistic questions regarding fully and precisely implementing the "one country, two systems" principle. It is safe to say that he has given us the best guidance on understanding the profound theory, logic and the laws for its daily exercise.

As an unprecedented system experiment, the implementation of "one country, two systems" is widely recognized as a great success, though, admittedly, not without some disruptions and sabotage by both internal and external hostile forces over the years. Looking ahead, we expect as many challenges, if not more, as Hong Kong does its best to handle the worsening geopolitical situation in the days to come. Having said that, we have the central authorities to thank for the foresight in promulgating the National Security Law for Hong Kong in 2020, followed by the National People's Congress' (NPC) decision to improve Hong Kong's electoral system through local legislation to ensure "patriots administering Hong Kong". Thus, Hong Kong successfully achieved the transition from severe social unrest to restoring order and rule of law in just two years, allowing the exercise of "one country, two systems" to proceed on the right track again.

Trailblazing system experiments are bound to run into setbacks and mistakes sooner or later, as has been proved true by the exercise of "one country, two systems" in the past 25 years. We have no doubt gained valuable experience and paid a dear price for it. In hindsight, the most important takeaways from 25 years of implementing "one country, two systems", in terms of better understanding its original intent and philosophy, should include the following:

First, upholding the sovereignty, national security and development interest of the country is the overriding principle of it all. "One country, two systems" is a system arrangement designed to facilitate the ultimate reunification and good governance of the Chinese nation, in that order. It is stated in the Preamble of the Basic Law of the HKSAR that the establishment of the HKSAR and the exercise of "one country, two systems" in the HKSAR are meant to uphold national reunification and territorial integrity as well as maintaining Hong Kong's long-term prosperity and stability. Similarly, the general secretary's report to the 18th National Congress of the Communist Party of China (CPC) also maintains that upholding the country's sovereignty, national security, development interest and Hong Kong's long-term prosperity and stability is the fundamental objective of "one country, two systems". The prerequisite for enjoying this system arrangement privilege is that Hong Kong must fulfill its constitutional obligation of upholding the sovereignty, national security and development interest of the country, especially securing the "three bottom lines" spelled out by President Xi Jinping.

Second, the Constitution of the People's Republic of China (PRC) and the Basic Law of the HKSAR together make up the constitutional foundation of the HKSAR. The Constitution is the basic law and supreme law of the country; while the Basic Law was made according to the Constitution. That means the Basic

Law cannot be explained outside the context of the Constitution, and the HKSAR does not have its own "constitutional order" or "rule of law" removed from the Constitution of the PRC. This constitutional foundation and order requires the HKSAR to adapt its social system and administration to the social system of the main body of the country. The HKSAR government and Hong Kong residents are required to respect and follow the spirit of the nation's Constitution and the leadership of the CPC, as well as to respect and uphold the socialist system of the country. Equally important is that Hong Kong society must uphold the authority of the Basic Law and ensure all its provisions are effectively enforced.

Third, the Central People's Government holds the right to maintain overall jurisdiction over the SARs and shall never be contradicted by the SARs' high degree of autonomy, which exists only because of the authorization of the Central People's Government in the first place. Hong Kong's high degree of autonomy is derived from the central government's overall jurisdiction over the SARs and therefore may never be separated from each other, or Hong Kong affairs will go awry. The SAR governments are accountable to the central authorities and subject to the latter's supervision. The central government holds the right to make final decisions over matters concerning the political system of the SARs; while the SAR governments are responsible for affairs within their respective jurisdiction.

Fourth, the SARs must always maintain an executive-led political structure and governance system. This is an extension of the previous point. When Hong Kong returned to the motherland 25 years ago, it automatically became an integral part of the nation's governance system again, and this time for good. The political system of the HKSAR must be effectively connected to the political system of the country's main body. The reality that Hong Kong implements an executive-led governing system is determined by the constitutional order that China is a unitary state and that the SAR status is derived from the Constitution. This constitutional arrangement ensures the chief executive is accountable to the central government. Hong Kong's constitutional development, therefore, must be conducive to the efficiency of the executive-led governance structure, ensures that the chief executive wields core leadership and authority over the SAR governance, and elevates the performance quality of the SAR government.

Fifth, we must ensure "patriots administering Hong Kong". "Patriots administering Hong Kong" defines "the people of Hong Kong administer Hong Kong", which is enshrined in the Basic Law of the HKSAR. That is why the Basic Law also stipulates that all public servants from the chief executive down swear allegiance to the Hong Kong Special Administrative Region of the People's Republic of China, and pledge to uphold the Basic Law of the Hong Kong Special Administrative Region of the People's Republic of China upon taking office. Hong Kong administrators must always keep the country in mind, while the electoral system of the SAR must ensure only sworn patriots are trusted with running the governance mechanism. Only then can we ensure Hong Kong's governance works effectively in maintaining its long-term prosperity and stability in the best interest of Hong Kong residents.

Sixth, we should maintain Hong Kong's unique constitutional status and advantages. Implementing "one country, two systems" means maintaining Hong Kong's characteristics and advantages to the best of our abilities in order to achieve the ultimate reunification of the Chinese nation. Hong Kong is in a unique position to serve the motherland as a "super-connector" while enjoying the unmatched support of the mainland. To capitalize on its unique role and for its future development, Hong Kong needs to integrate its own development into the country's overall development strategy. It is the best way to secure its irreplaceable role in contributing to the country's modernization, which in turn will benefit the city's socioeconomic development. Hong Kong stands to benefit immensely from playing its unique role in national development and the great rejuvenation of the Chinese nation.

The six points listed above are interconnected and consistent in demonstrating that "one country" precedes "two systems", and that "two systems" cannot exist without "one country". "One country, two systems" is a national policy based on the premise that the main body of the country maintains its socialist system, or there can be no "two systems" to speak of. In other words, the mainland is the main body of the country, and its socialist system predetermines the existence of "one country, two systems". Deng Xiaoping once famously said, "We exercise socialism with Chinese characteristics, which is why the 'one country, two systems' policy was created and why two systems are allowed to exist side by side." He also said, "Without the CPC or socialism with Chinese characteristics, no one can come up with such a policy." The uniqueness of "one country, two systems" lies in the fact that the socialist system of the main body of the country works alongside the capitalist system of the SARs, with the main body of the country having the SARs' back at all times and ensuring the latter's uniqueness thrives under such a unique system arrangement. That is why President Xi Jinping concluded recently, "The advantages of 'two systems' are as apparent only as much as the 'one country' principle is solid." This is the most important key to understanding "one country, two systems".

We can have a clearer vision of how "one country, two systems" will move on in the future by looking back to the past. There is no doubt that "one country, two systems" must be implemented comprehensively and faithfully, as President Xi Jinping has repeatedly emphasized, which means its fundamental principles must be upheld, whatever challenges it faces during its implementation.

That Hong Kong will have a bright future is as true as the notion that rivers and sky are eternal. The SAR is transitioning from order to prosperity after braving numerous storms along the way over the past 25 years. As long as we remain committed to the original intention of "one country, two systems" as the SAR advances with the times, it will write another splendid chapter in the practice of "one country, two systems" for sure.

The opening words: Let's revisit the original intent of "one country, two systems"

"A mission is accomplishable only if we remain committed to it." This is a simple truth fully illustrated by the implementation of "one country, two systems" in Hong Kong. The ultimate reason why it has encountered so many conflicts and challenges over the years is that the understanding and implementation of "one country, two systems" have been incomplete and inaccurate, deviating from its original intention. Therefore, it is imperative for Hong Kong to recall its original intent.

Back in October 1949, the People's Liberation Army (PLA) had taken control of South China and was very close to accomplishing the epic mission of "liberating the whole country", but stopped short of crossing the Shenzhen River into Hong Kong. No one was in doubt of the PLA's capability to defeat the British colonists and reclaim the city, but the central authorities decided to take it slow. In hindsight, that was no doubt a wise decision, as evidenced by the crucial role Hong Kong played throughout the formative years of the People's Republic amid ruthless attempts by Western powers to strangle the new China in its infancy. Hong Kong remained the only link between China's mainland and the outside world for decades, and became the most important source of overseas investment when the reform and opening-up drive began in the late 1970s.

In fact, the Chinese government is determined to achieve the complete reunification of the motherland by resolving the questions of Hong Kong, Macao and Taiwan in that order. It has never been a question of whether or not, but how to achieve that ultimate goal with minimum cost acceptable to most people. Deng Xiaoping put it very clearly: "The real question for China is how to solve the question of Hong Kong and Taiwan. There are only two options — by peaceful means and otherwise." He also concluded: "Whether Hong Kong will remain prosperous under China's jurisdiction ultimately depends on policies tailor-made for Hong Kong."

What is a "suitable policy for Hong Kong" then? After careful consideration, Deng came up with the great and innovative concept of "one country, two systems", a brand-new and feasible solution for the international community, as well as China, in resolving this kind of inherited problem. This is a departure from the usual ways of recovering lost territory through war, historically. This is a bold experiment in national governance and a significant contribution to human civilization.

"One country, two systems" was originally designed to resolve the question of Taiwan but ended up being applied to Hong Kong first. The rest is history. More than 20 years after China resumed the exercise of sovereign rule over Hong Kong, the "one country, two systems" principle has proved its effectiveness in sustaining Hong Kong's prosperity and stability, and gained recognition from the international community. Precisely because it proved workable, doable and popular, the US-based *Fortune* magazine, which declared not long before July 1, 1997 "Hong Kong is dead", admitted years later, "We were wrong."

"One country, two systems" is intended for facilitating national reunification and national governance. It deals with the reunification issue before Hong Kong's return to the motherland, and the governance of the special administrative region after Hong Kong's return. President Xi Jinping pointed out: "A nation that does not know where it came from has no idea where to go." Reflecting upon the past helps explain and resolve the questions at hand, including the questions of why the central government chose "one country, two systems" over "one country, one system"; why the central government exercises overall jurisdiction over

Hong Kong; why the governance of the SAR is led by the executive branch instead of having a separation of powers among the executive, legislative and judicial; whether it is true that nothing has changed after China resumed sovereign rule over Hong Kong; will "one country, two systems" prevail beyond 2047; why did the central authorities enacted the National Security Law for Hong Kong; and why must the precept of "patriots governing Hong Kong" be upheld, etc. Once these questions are answered, misunderstandings clarified, and confusing misinterpretations debunked, people will know what should be maintained, improved, corrected or abandoned. Only then will we be able to implement "one country, two systems" consistently and surely with increasing confidence and ease for as long as necessary.

The simplest way is usually the correct way. The next chapter of this series will discuss and straighten out the concept of "one country, two systems" by recalling its original intent.

Why was "one country, two systems" chosen?

Why was "one country, two systems" chosen? Were there other options in terms of system arrangements for Hong Kong? What was the rationale behind the Chinese government's decision to take back and govern Hong Kong under the "one country, two systems" principle?

Undoubtedly, there was sufficient jurisprudential grounds for China to implement "one country, one system" in Hong Kong upon resuming the exercise of sovereign rule over the city in 1997. Sovereignty is always accompanied by jurisdiction. Ever since China resumed the exercise of sovereign rule over Hong Kong, its central government has been authorized by the Constitution to exercise overall jurisdiction over the SAR. As the CPC is the sole governing party of the country, it is authorized by the Constitution to exercise overall jurisdiction over Hong Kong as it does over the rest of the country. That means China has every right to introduce the socialist system in Hong Kong if it chooses to replace the capitalist system and lifestyle under the British rule with its own socialist system and lifestyle after the resumption of sovereign rule over Hong Kong. A sovereign state can adopt any social system at its own discretion because it is a universal principle recognized by the international community.

However, the central government refused to do so. Instead, it set up a Special Administrative Region in Hong Kong and bestowed it a high degree of autonomy that allows Hong Kong people to govern Hong Kong. For this purpose, the NPC enacted the Basic Law of the Hong Kong Special Administrative Region of the People's Republic of China, which prescribes the relationships between the central government and the SAR, the rights and obligations of Hong Kong residents, and the scope of the SAR's autonomy; and promises to keep this framework unchanged for 50 years.

Choosing "one country, two systems" over "one country, one system", according to Deng Xiaoping, was a political decision "in full respect of Hong Kong's history and reality". The decision was accepted by all parties concerned because its original intent of preserving Hong Kong's unique advantages as much as possible under the premise of national reunification would let the city maintain its prosperity and stability after its return to China.

Li Ruihuan, former chairman of the Chinese People's Political Consultative Conference (CPPCC), once told Hong Kong and Macao members of the CPPCC a story about a used teapot. An elderly woman brought a used purple clay teapot that had been with her family for over a century to the flea market to sell for a fraction of one silver tael. An experienced antique buyer saw a thick layer of residue built up inside the teapot and knew it was worth much more than her asking price (in ancient China, people believed the older a purple clay teapot is and the more residue it contains, the better the tea in it tastes). So he offered almost ten times more in silver for the teapot and asked the elderly woman to wait for him while he went home to get more silver because he did not have enough on him. While waiting for the buyer, the elderly woman decided to make the teapot look better by thoroughly cleaning it up inside and out, much to the horror of the buyer. The story was Li's way of showing how much the central authorities value what Hong Kong has to offer and why Beijing chose to implement "one country, two systems" in the SAR.

Since Hong Kong had been separated from the motherland for so long, it had a hard time getting used to being a part of the family, given how different the motherland was from the United Kingdom. That was why the great majority of Hong Kong residents wanted the existing social system and lifestyle to remain unchanged, as did the central government. Back in the 1980s and 1990s, Hong Kong was already a regional center of international finance, trade and shipping with its own unique business environment, complete rule of law and worldwide connections unmatched by its mainland counterparts. Had China chosen "one country, one system" for Hong Kong, the latter would have become just another modern city, losing its splendor as the "Pearl of the East" for good. Hong Kong, thanks to its unique advantages as a free port and international financial center in the region, has played an irreplaceable role in the country's reform and opening-up. Keeping the existing social system and lifestyle would not only allow Hong Kong to remain prosperous and stable but continue playing its irreplaceable role in the nation's future development. It is a win-win formula. In Deng Xiaoping's words, "Hong Kong's prosperity and stability are closely linked to China's national development strategy." "It is in China's best interest to maintain the prosperity and stability of Hong Kong."

Why is "one country, two systems" an essential part of socialism with Chinese characteristics?

The Basic Law of the HKSAR stipulates that Hong Kong will not exercise socialism as the main body of the nation does after its return to the motherland, and its capitalist system and existing way of life will remain unchanged for 50 years. The then-State leader Deng Xiaoping also said back in the day that "one country, two systems" was "a very important part" of socialism with Chinese characteristics. How should we make sense of these notions?

Deng gave as his reasoning a fact: The main body of China exercises socialism with Chinese characteristics, which allowed the "one country, two systems" arrangement to be introduced in the first place. What is socialism with Chinese characteristics? Simply put, it is "socialism" combined with "Chinese characteristics", meaning the country adheres to the basic theory of socialism while blazing its own socialist path suited to its actual conditions and national interest. Practices such as reform and opening-up, a socialist market economy, co-existence of different forms of ownership, and various methods of wealth distribution being employed at the same time are all different from the previous, rigid school of socialism we knew in the past, and they make up the socialism with Chinese characteristics we exercise today. Similarly, "one country, two systems" was created by the CPC to better facilitate the national development strategy with Hong Kong's history and present condition in mind. It is the outcome of seeking truth from real life (or pragmatism at work) and therefore may appear at odds with the classical definition of socialism in terms of system arrangement. Deng once said, "Our social system is socialism with Chinese characteristics, which is demonstrated in part by how we handle the question of reunification with Hong Kong, Macao and Taiwan, namely, through 'one country, two systems'","Ours is socialism with Chinese characteristics, which is why we introduced the 'one country, two systems' policy so that the two systems can exist side by side".

There are three points of significance in understanding "one country, two systems" as an essential part of socialism with Chinese characteristics. First, one system comes before the other when we talk about "two systems": The practice of "socialism with Chinese characteristics" on the mainland is the precondition for Hong Kong to maintain a capitalist system. "One country, two systems" was created on the precondition that the main body of the nation — the mainland — will always exercise socialism, or "one country, two systems" would not have been possible. Second, the capitalist system of the HKSAR must operate in a way that is in harmony with the socialist system of the mainland. Hong Kong's system is not one that belongs to an independent political entity and must not work against the socialist system of the mainland. Rather, it should adapt to and harmonize with the mainland's socialist system. Third, Hong Kong's capitalist system will remain unchanged only when the socialist system of the mainland remains unchanged. Deng Xiaoping said it best when he laid down this rule: "In order to keep Hong Kong's prosperity and stability for 50 years and beyond, the country must maintain its socialist system under the leadership of the CPC."

Explaining why "one country, two systems" is an essential part of socialism with Chinese characteristics does not mean we want to replace Hong Kong's capitalist system with the mainland's socialist system. On the contrary, the goal is to boost Hong Kong's socioeconomic development while facilitating the country's development, which is crucial to Hong Kong's development after all. To build up socialism with Chinese characteristics, we need to learn from the great achievements of other civilizations around the world, and Hong Kong should play an important role in the process. Thus "one country, two systems" serves the national development strategy perfectly. As Deng explained back in the day, "The main body of China must practice socialism, but the practice of capitalism is allowed in some parts of the country." "Letting a capitalist system exist in a small region should facilitate socialist development better."

The CPC is the leader of socialism with Chinese characteristics and therefore also the leader of "one county, two systems". Under the leadership of the CPC, socialism with Chinese characteristics allows the existence of capitalism in a small region of the country as long as it contributes to national development. That is why the CPC Central Committee regards "one country, two systems" as an outstanding advantage of the country's social system and governance system as well as one of the basic strategies for maintaining and developing socialism with Chinese characteristics in the new era.

Why is "crossing the river by feeling the stones" necessary?

"Cross the river by feeling the stones." These words of wisdom have been passed down for generations and inspired the Chinese nation in the early days of the reform and opening-up in the late 1970s and early '80s. Since "one country, two systems" is unprecedented in human history, the only way to implement it successfully is by trial and error, at least in the beginning. That is why Deng Xiaoping described it as "crossing the river by feeling the stones".

The Communist Party of China reached the conclusion, at the fourth plenary session of its 19th Central Committee in October 2019, "The 'one country, two systems' principle is an integral institutional arrangement adopted by the CPC in leading the people toward the peaceful reunification of the motherland, as well as a great innovation of socialism with Chinese characteristics." That spoke highly of "one country, two systems" regarding its significance and historical role.

As a matter of fact, "one country, two systems" can be interpreted from different perspectives. In terms of difficulty of implementation, the Fourth Plenary Session of the 16th CPC Central Committee described it as a "brand new challenge" for the CPC in national governance. The 17th CPC National Congress elevated it to a "major challenge". In terms of guiding theory on governance, the 19th CPC National Congress listed maintaining "one country, two systems" as one of the fourteen fundamental strategies in governing the country in the new era of upholding and developing socialism with Chinese characteristics. In terms of its nature and characteristics, the Fourth Plenary Session of the 19th CPC Central Committee named it one of the thirteen outstanding advantages of China's institutions and governance philosophy.

Those descriptions may be different, but there is a clear logic: It is unprecedented because it was a great innovation; it is a brand new challenge because it is unprecedented; it needs to be improved constantly because it is an important, fundamental strategy in national governance; and we have full confidence in it because it is an outstanding advantage that we ought to maintain as long as it is necessary.

China did not have prior experience in anything like "one

country, two systems", the implementation of which began only when China resumed the exercise of sovereign rule over Hong Kong on July 1, 1997. In early 20th century, the CPC established its own Soviet-style government in such regions as Hunan province, Jiangxi province and northern Shanxi province, complete with its own rule of law and currency. Although they earned the distinction of "clear sky" for corruption-free governance, they were "illegal" in the eyes of the Kuomintang (the Chinese Nationalist Party) regime, which spared no effort in wiping out the CPC — in sharp contrast to today's Hong Kong, which enjoys a high degree of autonomy with unmatched protection and support from the nation prescribed by the Basic Law. Around the world, no regions that have been granted a certain level of autonomy have in place institutions different from that of the rest of the country — as opposed to what the unique principle of "one country, two systems" has made possible.

At its 16th National Congress, the CPC gave credit to two turning points when its political role changed historically. One happened on October 1, 1949, when the PRC was born and the CPC turned from a political party fighting to seize state power to the governing party set to maintain state governance as long as necessary. The other one was witnessed when reform and opening-up officially started in 1978, as the CPC proceeded to replace its old style of state governance catering to a closed and planned national economy with a new style of governance suitable for the long-term development of a market-oriented economy. Come to think of it, it is fair to see Hong Kong's return to the motherland as yet another turning point in the CPC's progression as the governing party of China. That was when the CPC decided to maintain a capitalist, free economy in part of the country while continuing to pursue socialism with Chinese characteristics in the main body of the country. The latest turning point may not be as significant as the previous two, but qualifies as an unprecedented and brand-new test for the Party in its own right.

By the same token, "one country, two systems" is a bona fide challenge for Hong Kong as well. Deng Xiaoping once said, "'one country, two systems' is a new undertaking for all of us and no one is sure how it will fare down the road." Since none of us can actually see the future, both the central government and the SAR need to keep studying the exercise of "one country, two systems" inside out. By doing so, we will build our knowledge from the ground up and tackle each problem as it pops up along the way. Be it 50 years or longer, the practice of "one country, two systems" would inevitably encounter twists and turns; we should explore and grasp the practical rules step by step. With the practice and understanding of "one country, two systems" deepening gradually, the framework will continue to improve, facilitating smoother implementation in the future.

Why must "one country, two systems" be viewed from two perspectives?

"One country, two systems" is an integral concept. That "one country" precedes "two systems" lays bare their primary and secondary relation and inseparability. To accurately define the framework and the relationship between the two, we must touch on two aspects.

As stated in the preamble of the Basic Law, the implementation of "one country, two systems" is aimed at upholding national unity and territorial integrity, as well as maintaining the prosperity and stability of Hong Kong. But the promotion and presentation of "one country, two systems" was incomplete during a long period in the past. There was an overemphasis on"Hong Kong people governing Hong Kong"and "a high degree of autonomy"while the central government's jurisdiction over the HKSAR and the relationship between"two systems" were downplayed; and it was stressed that the central government would not intervene in while providing

Hong Kong dependable support whenever necessary. "Two systems" was simplistically interpreted as "the well water does not mix with the river water". Such assertions are incomplete, though not completely faulty, and could lead to an overemphasis on one system at the expense of the other one over time, thus hindering the shaping of correct "one country, two systems" values.

What "well water must not intrude into river water" really means is that the mainland will not impose socialism on Hong Kong and Hong Kong should not force capitalism upon the mainland. It should not be interpreted as "two systems" being irrelevant. Those with ulterior motives have resisted the central government's powers, tried to cut "two systems" apart and reject "one country" under the guise of "anti-intervention". This is a typical manifestation of the chaos caused by the deviation from the original intent of "one country, two systems" after the return of Hong Kong.

The mainland and Hong Kong are two sides of the same coin; so are the central government and the HKSAR government. Safeguarding national sovereignty, security and development interests is the overriding principle of the "one country, two systems" principle. Keen observers should have noticed that ever since the convening of the 18th CPC National Congress, "one country, two systems" has been elaborated on from both the national and Hong Kong perspectives. For instance, that "the fundamental purpose is to safeguard national sovereignty, security and development interests, maintain the long-term prosperity and stability in Hong Kong and Macao" was emphasized in the 18th CPC National Congress; "exercise the central government's power in accordance with the law, ensure a high degree of autonomy in accordance with the law" in the Fourth Plenary Session of the 18th CPC Central Committee; "it is imperative for the central government's overall jurisdiction over the Hong Kong and Macao SARs and the two SARs' high degree of autonomy to be melded in an organic way" in the 19th CPC National Congress. These expressions share a common feature, that is, the "country" comes before "Hong Kong". In other words, "two systems" exists only when "one country" exists; and national interests must be given top priority when implementing "one country, two systems".

The central government has repeatedly emphasized that "one country, two systems" must be implemented accurately and fully. At the ceremony marking the 20th anniversary of Hong Kong's return to the motherland, President Xi Jinping elaborated on the relationship between "one country" and "two systems". "'One country' is the premise and basis of 'two systems', and 'two systems' is subordinate to and derived from 'one country'." "'One country' is like the roots of a tree. For a tree to grow tall and luxuriant, its roots must run deep and strong", Xi explained. His remarks should have helped people correctly understand the relationship between "one country" and "two systems", and clarified the authentic definition of the framework.

By logical extension, "adhering to the 'one country' principle while respecting the differences between 'two systems'", "making full use of the motherland's support and the SAR's competitive edges" and "making good use of the advantages of 'one country, two systems' " — expressions like these are all derived from the same principle.

Deng Xiaoping had repeatedly reminded Hong Kong people: The socialist mainland is both the main body and foundation of the "one country, two systems" framework; "it wouldn't work without this premise". "Hong Kong's prosperity and stability wouldn't last if the country's main body has its political institution changed", and "'one country, two systems' wouldn't be possible without giving full consideration to these two aspects".

Why was Hong Kong not a colony of Britain before 1997?

Before 1997, Britain regarded Hong Kong as its "overseas territory", an alias for colony. However, Hong Kong was in fact not a colony; it was merely under the colonial rule of the British. It is very important to note the difference, which will help us understand the significance of Hong Kong's return to the motherland and see the ulterior motives of Britain's "glorious retreat" as well as the absurdity of Hong Kong independence.

In the eyes of British colonists, Hong Kong Island and the Kowloon Peninsula were "permanently ceded", thus Britain had sovereignty over these two territories. Even though the New Territories was leased for 99 years, "the empire on which the sun never set" did not need to worry about giving it back to China, a poor and crumbling nation back then. Without a doubt, the British government ran Hong Kong as a colony in the capacity of suzerain.

However, that was just their assumption. No Chinese government since the demise of the 1911 Revolution (Xinhai Revolution) recognized the unfair treaties that ceded Hong Kong to the United Kingdom and gave up China's sovereignty over Hong Kong. Soon after the PRC took over the country's seat at the United Nations in October 1971, it wrote to the United Nations Special Committee on Decolonization and solemnly declared that both Hong Kong and Macao are Chinese territories that were occupied by the UK and Portugal respectively under a series of unequal treaties they had forced the Qing Dynasty's rulers to sign. The letter also states that resolving the questions of Hong Kong and Macao is a matter within China's sovereignty; the two cities must not be treated as "colonies" in the usual sense of the word. A month later, the UN General Assembly passed a resolution by a vote of 99 : 5 that removed Hong Kong and Macao from the list of existing colonies. By doing so, China reconfirmed a historical fact and reaffirmed its sovereignty beyond a reasonable doubt.

Independence movements swept across colonies after World War II, some of which changed their relationship with their former suzerains forever, and declared their independence to become sovereign states. Hong Kong was not one of them, however, because it was not a colony to begin with, it was a Chinese territory to be taken back, and China has never handed its sovereignty over the territory to another country. Therefore, ideas such as sovereignty and national independence are not applicable to Hong Kong. By removing Hong Kong from the UN list of non-self-governing territories, China effectively eliminated any sovereignty dispute and cleared the path for Hong Kong's return to the motherland. That is why neither the *Sino-British Joint Declaration* nor the Basic Law contains the words "resuming sovereignty (over Hong Kong)" or "return of sovereignty". Instead, they use the words "resuming the exercise of sovereignty (over Hong Kong)". The Basic Law illuminates this issue at the very beginning, as its preamble starts with "Hong Kong has been part of the territory of China since ancient times", and Article 1 says "the Hong Kong Special Administrative Region is an inalienable part of the People's Republic of China".

Britain, the old imperial power, has never left its former colonies a clean slate when its rule approached its end. It always pursued "glorious retreat" by force-feeding its colonies with crude democratic elections that tended to divide rather than unite the society, allowing the former colonial master to maintain its influence there forever. As a result, those newly independent nations have long suffered from social unrest and weak government. Likewise, the British Hong Kong government played this trick during the lead-up to its departure. Christopher Patten, the last British governor of Hong Kong, initiated an electoral cram course that he has proudly described as a process of turning the city into a democracy. In doing so, he single-handedly destroyed the "through-train" arrangement for the city's old legislature to become the Legislative Council (LegCo) of the HKSAR. Britain denied Hong Kong society any form of democracy for well over a century before it signed the *Sino-British Joint Declaration* with China in 1984. Then in a great rush, it launched a process to "hand the government back to the people". Many cannot help but suspect what Britain really wanted for Hong Kong was self-determination instead of democracy.

As for an assortment of pro-independence fantasies that popped up in recent years — such as "Hong Kong as a city-state", "Hong Kong as a nation" and "self-determination", along with ridiculous demonstrations of love for the colonial past — all are illusionary ideas divorced from reality with no legal basis.

Why does the central government have overall jurisdiction over Hong Kong?

The White Paper on "The Practice of the 'One Country, Two Systems' Policy in the Hong Kong Special Administrative Region", issued in June 2014 by the Information Office of the State Council, states that the central government holds the power to exercise overall jurisdiction in the HKSAR. This statement of a plain fact irritated some people in the city who interpreted "overall jurisdiction" as "controlling everything", "one country, one system" and even "unauthorized addition" to the Basic Law of the HKSAR. Such accusations are absurd at best and indicative of their ignorance regarding the relationship between the central government and the HKSAR.

"Overall jurisdiction" is not difficult to comprehend. It represents the inherent authority of the sovereign state and is not in conflict with the high degree of autonomy of the SAR. Nor does it mean the central government controls everything in Hong Kong.

Why is the power of "overall jurisdiction" the "inherent authority" of the central government? Historically speaking, no Chinese government after the 1911 Revolution (Xinhai Revolution) abandoned sovereignty over Hong Kong, although the state was unable to exercise jurisdiction because the city was occupied by the British Empire. With the resumption of the exercise of sovereignty over Hong Kong, the Chinese government naturally regained the governing power of the SAR. President Xi Jinping made it clear, "Hong Kong has been back in the national governance system since China resumed the exercise of sovereignty over the city." Sovereignty is demonstrated through overall jurisdiction. It would be pointless to resume the exercise of sovereignty over Hong Kong without the power to exercise overall jurisdiction over the HKSAR.

Why is "overall jurisdiction" not in conflict with a "high degree of autonomy"? Under "one country, two systems", the SAR enjoys a high degree of autonomy, within which it manages the local affairs. That a high degree of autonomy is implemented in the SAR represents a unique way in which the central government's overall jurisdiction over the SAR is exercised, or, to put it another way, the SAR's high degree of autonomy is an organic component of the central government's overall jurisdiction, which is exercised, to a large extent, through the

SAR's high degree of autonomy.

Sovereignty is the ultimate decision-making power, the highest authority of the state to handle domestic and foreign affairs independently and on its own accord. As a unitary state, China's sovereignty is exclusively maintained by the State rather than being shared with regional authorities. Overall jurisdiction cannot be separated from sovereignty, because sovereignty is the basis of overall jurisdiction and makes the latter legitimate; meanwhile exercising overall jurisdiction is how sovereignty manifests itself, meaning sovereignty without overall jurisdiction is just an empty idea. The central government exercises sovereign power and determines the way it runs Hong Kong, including a political framework that ensures its sovereign power and overall jurisdiction, which is the main reason why the SAR's institutions are led by the executive branch.

When Margaret Thatcher visited China and during the subsequent negotiations between China and the United Kingdom on the future of Hong Kong, the British side attempted to continue usurping the exercise of sovereignty over the city by trying to confirm the effectiveness of the unequal treaties. After Deng Xiaoping rejected such proposals, the UK government offered China a "deal" that would give the exercise of sovereignty over Hong Kong back to China while Britain keeps the right to exercise overall jurisdiction over the city. It was of course categorically rejected by the Chinese side, as Deng insisted "the people of Hong Kong can take good care of their city on their own".

Some people assume "one country, two systems" means the central government holds sovereignty over Hong Kong while overall jurisdiction belongs to the latter. Their logic is the same as that of "sovereignty in exchange for overall jurisdiction" proposed by Britain, which would have severed sovereignty and overall jurisdiction over Hong Kong. The establishment of SARs and implementation of "one country, two systems" do not affect China's unitary state model that features a unitary sovereignty, one constitution and one central government. Hong Kong's high degree of autonomy is not inherent. Without the power to exercise overall jurisdiction, the sovereign State could not have authorized a high degree of autonomy for the HKSAR. Meanwhile, the central government fully respects and firmly upholds the special administrative region's high degree of autonomy.

The white paper states that the overall jurisdiction includes the powers exercised directly by the central authorities, including the power to grant the SAR a high degree of autonomy. The central authorities also have the power to supervise the SAR's exercise of its high degree of autonomy. The central authorities exercise their powers at their own discretion; the SAR exercises its powers under the supervision of the central authorities; the powers are exercised in accordance with the law and in the way they should be; both the duties and the powers are carried out in the proper way. That is what the central authorities did.

Why are the central government's overall jurisdiction over the SARs and their high degree of autonomy a coherent whole?

The central government's overall jurisdiction over the two special administrative regions of Hong Kong and Macao and the high degree of autonomy the two SARs enjoy by authorization of the central government are designed as a coherent system, and the logic behind it is all about national governance and regional governance functioning organically. It serves the need of the SAR system to work effectively according to the "one country, two systems" principle.

The Hong Kong and Macao SARs enjoy administrative, legislative and independent judicial powers by authorization, as well as the power of final adjudication, and this constitutional order defines the high degree of autonomy the two SARs enjoy under "one country, two systems". Furthermore, the central government holds the right and power to oversee the exercise of "one country, two systems" in accordance with the respective

Basic Law of the two SARs, which specifies what affairs related to the SARs are the central government's responsibility and what falls under the SAR jurisdiction, as well as the constitutional status of the SARs and their relationship with the central government. Such is the constitutional order of the SARs assigned by the Constitution of the PRC and the Basic Law, which was promulgated by the NPC in accordance with the Constitution. By virtue of the constitutional order of the SARs, the central government's overall jurisdiction over the SARs and the latter's high degree of autonomy are an organic and coherent dual; the SARs' high degree of autonomy cannot work properly without the central government's overall jurisdiction over the SARs.

The central government's overall jurisdiction over the SARs is more clearly demonstrated in Article 31 and Article 62 of the nation's Constitution, which stipulates that the NPC shall decide the establishment of the SARs and the systems to be instituted there. The Constitution and the Basic Law also stipulate the rights and powers the central government holds over specific SAR affairs, including the NPC's right to amend the Basic Law; the NPC Standing Committee's right to interpret the Basic Law, to decide and modify the method of selecting the chief executives and electing the legislative councils of the SARs, to keep a record of the legislative decisions reached by the legislative councils and send them back when necessary, to declare a state of emergency in the SARs, and give the SARs new authorizations; the State Council's right to appoint the chief executives of the SARs and principal officials of the SAR governments, to handle foreign affairs related to the SARs and issue orders to the chief executives; and the Central Military Committee's right to deploy and command the PLA units in the SARs and its responsibility over national defense-related matters. In 2006, the NPC Standing Committee authorized Hong Kong to exercise jurisdiction over the "Hong Kong port area" within the Shenzhen Bay Port in accordance with the laws of the SAR. This was a new authorization.

"High degree of autonomy" is not full autonomy or a decentralized power but the power to run local affairs as authorized by the central government. There is no "residual power" beside the power authorized by the central government. By constitutional design, central government authorization does not limit or restrict the central government's overall jurisdiction over the SARs. The overall jurisdiction is a sovereign power reserved for the State, from which the high degree of autonomy of the SARs is derived. The "high degree of autonomy" must uphold the "overall jurisdiction" and never defy or oppose it. Some provisions of the Basic Law are not only intended to ensure the high degree of autonomy but also supervise the implementation of the Basic Law in the SAR. For example, every law passed by the LegCo of each SAR must be submitted to the NPC for archiving, and any law that is rejected by the NPC is automatically null and void. Also, the NPC Standing Committee holds the right to interpret the Basic Law but may authorize the courts of the SAR to interpret specific provisions of the Basic Law when adjudicating cases.

Hong Kong has returned to the nation's governance system since the PRC resumed the exercise of sovereign rule over it 25 years ago and, by virtue of its constitutional order, Hong Kong's high degree of autonomy is naturally tied to the central government's overall jurisdiction over the SAR and cannot be effective without the latter. That is the only way to ensure that Hong Kong's overall interest is tied to the nation's fundamental interest forever. It is decidedly wrong to view the central government's overall jurisdiction over Hong Kong as infringing upon the high degree of autonomy of the SAR. Deng Xiaoping once said, "The central authorities for sure do not intervene in matters within the SAR's jurisdiction but must do so when the matters at hand concern national interest." He added that "the central authorities cannot afford letting go of all rights and powers over Hong Kong affairs, or chaos may emerge and Hong Kong's interests may be harmed". Therefore, it is in Hong Kong's interest for the central government to retain certain powers over the SAR. The enactment of the National Security Law for Hong Kong and the overhaul of its electoral system proved Deng was absolutely correct when he predicted, "There are always some things (Hong Kong) cannot solve without the central government's help."

Why is an executive-led system prescribed for Hong Kong?

The governance model of Hong Kong, though different from that of the Chinese mainland, is part of the national governance system and thus should be compatible with the political structure of the nation. For this reason, an executive-led system is prescribed by the Basic Law for the HKSAR.

The then-State leader Deng Xiaoping said, "The stability of Hong Kong hinges not only on economic development but also a stable political system." "We must design our system and administrative model based on our actual conditions." It was the most strenuous work to design a political structure for the HKSAR in the whole process of drafting the Basic Law. From the central government's perspective, the political structure must provide it with a mechanism to maintain its sovereign power over the HKSAR, or the proposed high degree of autonomy would become full autonomy; an executive system with the chief executive provides the best of such mechanisms. From Hong Kong's perspective, the political structure must be conducive to retaining what has made Hong Kong successful in the past to maintain the city's stability and prosperity after the reunification; the executive-led arrangement is no doubt among the significant elements that have contributed to Hong Kong's past success, therefore it can be retained after some modifications.

According to the Basic Law, the central authorities supervise the executive, legislature and judiciary in the HKSAR in different ways and dimensions. Hong Kong has an independent judiciary, and members of the LegCo are elected by local electorates; whereas the locally-elected Chief Executive must be appointed by the central government. Likewise, the HKSAR's principal officials are appointed by the central government after they are nominated by the chief executive, who must also carry out the directives issued by the central government. The chief executive is the head and representative of the HKSAR, and is also the head of the HKSAR government who is in charge of the executive branch. The chief executive is accountable to both the HKSAR and the central government, and is obligated to pay annual duty visits to Beijing. The design of "dual function" and "dual accountability" for the post of the chief executive is so unique in the SAR's establishment that it highlights the authority of the chief executive and the dominance of the executive authorities in the governance system.

Obviously, it is the executive branch that is the most direct interface between the HKSAR and central government. The central government maintains its overall jurisdiction over Hong Kong based on the Basic Law, and mainly relies on the chief executive and the HKSAR government led by the chief executive in doing so. The notion that the central government relies on the Basic Law and the chief executive to govern Hong Kong is not without a reason. Some scholars who participated in the design of the HKSAR's political system referred to Hong Kong's political system as the "chief executive-accountable system". This is the significance and role of executive leadership in Hong Kong and in "one country, two systems".

In short, Hong Kong's execution-led system with the chief executive as the core is determined by China's unitary state structure and the HKSAR's constitutional status as a local administrative region directly under the central government. It is an effective way for the chief executive to be accountable to the central government.

Although the Basic Law does not contain the term "executive-led system", "Political Structure" highlights the dominance of the executive authorities by prescribing the functions of the chief executive, the executive authorities, the legislature, the judiciary, district organizations and public servants in that order. This arrangement is distinct from those of many countries and regions whose constitutional documents put their legislature ahead of the executive branch. This deliberate distinction unmistakably reflects the legislative intent of prescribing an executive-led system for the HKSAR. Article 64 of the Basic Law merely refers to the four specific scopes as enumerated after the colon therein. It does not mean that the HKSAR is subordinate to the LegCo.

On the 10th and 20th anniversary of the enactment of the Basic Law, the then-NPCSC chairmen Wu Bangguo and Zhang Dejiang noted that the unique design of the executive-led system is compatible with the SAR's constitutional status. They said that such a design meets the needs of the city as an international commercial and financial center for good governance. The executive-led system, which retains what has worked well in the old system, "is the best system for the sustainable development of Hong Kong". President Xi Jinping has also emphasized that the HKSAR must adhere to the executive-led system.

Why is Hong Kong's political system not one of "separation of powers"?

The political system established under the Hong Kong Letters Patent and Hong Kong Royal Instructions during British rule was not one of "separation of powers"; neither is the one established under the Basic Law of the HKSAR after reunification. Rather, both are executive-led systems. What sets them apart is that power was centralized in the executive branch before 1997, whereas for the executive-led model adopted after reunification, the executive and the legislature work in coordination with checks and balances.

In contrast with the Westminster model the United Kingdom had been practicing at home, it chose to centralize all power in the hands of the governors or even resorted to an authoritarian approach in its colonial rule over the territories it occupied overseas. In Hong Kong before reunification, the British monarch appointed the governor, who nominated and, upon the approval of the Foreign and Commonwealth Office, appointed members of both the executive and legislature as well as other senior offices. In effect, the governor centralized all power over both the executive and legislature in his hands by also serving as the president of the LegCo. During some 150 years of British rule, Hong Kong's political system transited from one allowing authoritarian executive power to one allowing the centralization of all power in the hands of the executive, and then to an executive-led model allowing elections on a very limited scale.

Christopher Patten, the last governor of Hong Kong, launched a wave of radical political reforms. In the name of accelerating democratic development, Patten was in effect trying to give more power to the legislature at the expense of the executive branch, creating trouble for executive-led governance after 1997. Qian Qichen, the then-Vice Premier and Minister of Foreign Affairs, sharply pointed out that Christopher Patten attempted to drastically change Hong Kong's governance system, turning its executive-led system into a legislature-led system.

Modern societies have three kinds of public power, namely the executive, legislative and judicial power; their relationship with each other varies across the globe. Hong Kong's governance model has the shape of "separation of powers", but the executive branch is vividly in a more authoritative position and plays a more active role in governance. The SAR government has the right of legislative initiative; government bills take priority on the agenda of the LegCo, the enactment of which requires only a simple majority vote whereas LegCo members' bills have a higher bar to pass. According to Article 74 of the Basic Law, lawmakers cannot introduce bills relating to public expenditure, political structure or the operation of the government; they can introduce bills relating to government policies only after securing the written consent of the chief executive. Unfortunately, this Article has not been effectively enforced. The executive branch can also impose checks and supervision on the judiciary: The chief executive has the authority to appoint and remove court judges in accordance with legal procedures. The chief executive also has the authority to remit or commute sentences meted out by judges; and the certificates issued by the chief executive on questions of fact concerning acts of state are binding on the courts.

Effective governance ensures social stability and development; and the political system is to ensure effective governance. In March 1990, when the NPC was deliberating the Basic Law, the Basic Law Drafting Committee emphasized that "the executive and the legislature should maintain checks and balances while coordinating with each other. To maintain Hong Kong's stability and administrative efficiency, the chief executive must have real power that at the same time should be subject to checks and supervision". Distinct from the executive-led model, which centralized all power in the hands of the governors under British rule, the Basic Law prescribes a political system featuring an executive-led governance model, an independent judiciary and mechanisms to facilitate checks and balances between the executive branch and the legislature, which also work in coordination, with the aim of establishing an efficient government amid democratic participation and democratic supervision. Some scholars in Hong Kong refer to it as "separation of powers under an executive-led system".

Deng Xiaoping once said many years ago that "Hong Kong's system cannot be fully westernized. It cannot copy the West's system." "It is inappropriate to use 'separation of powers' or Britain's parliamentary system as the standard of democracy". Executive-led, legislature-led and separation of powers are distinct models of governance. The United States' system is a typical model of separation of powers with the three branches of government forming a system of checks and balances. In the US Constitution, the Congress comes before the president and the judiciary. The UK operates politically under a legislature-led system or a parliamentary system, where the executive power is in the hands of the majority party in the parliament. Both the legislature-led and "separation of powers" models are only suitable for sovereign states; they are not appropriate political structures for regional administrations under a central government. As a special administrative region of China, Hong Kong can only adopt an executive-led governance model. "Separation of powers" is out of the question.

Why should we adhere to "patriots administering Hong Kong"?

"The people of Hong Kong administer Hong Kong" is a major characteristic of "one country, two systems", which is why the central government has not sent an official to Hong Kong as the head of the HKSAR government or a policy bureau since its return to the motherland. However, "the people of Hong Kong administer Hong Kong" has its own gist and limits, as does the high degree of autonomy of Hong Kong. High degree of autonomy, by definition, is not full autonomy. For the same reason "the people of Hong Kong administer Hong Kong" means Hong Kong must be administered by true patriots.

Deng Xiaoping made it clear back in the day that "'the people of Hong Kong administer Hong Kong' comes with a precondition, which is that Hong Kong must be administered by predominantly patriotic people". In the administration of the future SAR government, "there is only one condition for all participants: they must be patriots". What is the criterion of a patriot? According to Deng, "Patriots must respect their own nation, sincerely uphold the motherland's resumption of the exercise of sovereign rule over Hong Kong, and do not cause harm to Hong Kong's prosperity and stability." He gave that answer back in 1984, meaning "one country, two systems" was given the precondition of "patriots administering Hong Kong" from the very start of this framework's design process. Article 104 of the Basic Law of the HKSAR stipulates that when assuming office the principal officials, members of the Legislative Council, judges of the courts and other officeholders must swear to uphold the Basic Law of the Hong Kong Special Administrative Region of the People's Republic of China and swear allegiance to the Hong Kong Special Administrative Region of the People's Republic of China. That also embodies the principle of "patriots administering Hong Kong".

"Governance by patriots" is a common principle observed around the world, because no country would knowingly let unpatriotic people hold the governing power of the country or a region for that matter. As a matter of fact, all countries require civil servants to swear allegiance to the state and/or constitution; and the United Kingdom has a law forbidding "traitors" from standing in parliamentary elections. Both the Senate and the House of

Representatives of the US Congress have ethics committees that monitor lawmakers for disloyalty to the Union. The SAR's governance institutions are part of the state institutions, and patriotism is the basic political ethics of the SAR's government functionary. Our central government would never let unpatriotic people, much less sworn enemies of the state, seize the governing power of the HKSAR. It goes without saying that those who hold important powers and assume major responsibilities of governance must be staunch patriots.

In the past, an alarming number of anti-China subversives, including known advocates of separatism, infiltrated into the SAR's governance institutions such as the LegCo through elections; they hindered the SAR government's governance, resisted the central government's overall jurisdiction, and harmed the well-being of the Hong Kong public. They even came up with a set of detailed "mutual destruction" strategies to seize the governing power of the SAR by grabbing the majority of seats in LegCo and the Election Committee. They took advantage of the loopholes in the old electoral system, which explains why the central authorities had to plug those loopholes by revamping Hong Kong's electoral system to ensure the "patriots administering Hong Kong" principle is strictly observed by keeping all subversives at bay. Ensuring "patriots administering

Hong Kong" by means of law, the core objective of the electoral system revamp initiated by the NPC and implemented in 2021, eventually achieved the ultimate goal of perfecting a democratic electoral system best suited to Hong Kong's intrinsic sociopolitical condition. Call it democracy with Hong Kong characteristics if you will.

The revamped electoral system of the HKSAR, with an optimized eligibility review mechanism to prevent unpatriotic individuals from entering the governance structure, not only ensures staunch patriots are elected to hold important public offices but also broadens the representativeness of the Election Committee and improves the composition of functional constituencies to better enable public participation in the best interest of society as a whole. By authorizing the Election Committee to elect the chief executive and 40 of the 90 LegCo members, the improved electoral system will facilitate a healthy relationship between the executive and legislative branches of the HKSAR government and ensure executive-led administration of the HKSAR for more efficient governance. The improved electoral system does not exclude those who disagree with the HKSAR government as long as they qualify as patriots.

Hong Kong's transition from chaos to order has revealed a profound truth: "Patriots administering Hong Kong" is the guarantee for the smooth and sustainable implementation of "one country, two systems", President Xi Jinping noted on January 27, 2021 when the then-Chief Executive, Carrie Lam Cheng Yuet-ngor, delivered annual reporting of work. "It is a cardinal principle that is crucial to ensuring national sovereignty, security and development interests as well the long-term stability and prosperity of Hong Kong", Xi added. It is a cardinal principle because the proper relationship between "one country" and "two systems", the central government's overall jurisdiction over the SAR, and the constitutional order prescribed by the Constitution and the Basic Law cannot be sustained without the premise of "governance by patriots".

Why is the statutory basis of the Basic Law not the *Sino-British Joint Declaration?*

The Basic Law of the HKSAR was promulgated after China and Britain signed the *Sino-British Joint Declaration* on the Question of Hong Kong and has elaborated on the 12 basic principles and policies regarding Hong Kong that China listed in the *Joint Declaration.* That is why some people argue that the Basic Law is to some extent a derivative of the *Joint Declaration* and Britain, therefore, has the right to monitor the implementation of "one country, two systems" in Hong Kong in accordance with the *Joint Declaration.* But are they correct in saying so?

Let's not forget the *Joint Declaration* contains separate statements by the Chinese government and by its United Kingdom counterpart as well as their joint statements. The *Joint Declaration* was written this way because the two governments agreed on certain points but not on others. Thus, it was necessary to include points they agreed on and those they did not agree on in the *Joint Declaration*. Regarding Hong Kong's return to the motherland in 1997, the Chinese government declared that it had decided to "resume the exercise of sovereignty over Hong Kong", whereas the UK government declared that it would "restore Hong Kong to the People's Republic of China". Such an arrangement is indeed an ingenious way of dealing with the question by avoiding any ambiguity while taking into account each side's stance. As it turned out, the *Joint Declaration* consists of three parts: namely, 1) confirming that China would resume the exercise of sovereignty over Hong Kong; 2) the fundamental policies the Chinese government would be implementing in Hong Kong after its return to the motherland; 3) the arrangements for the transitional period before Hong Kong officially returned to the motherland. The UK government had the right and responsibility to implement the first and third parts, which have been completed. The second part is the Chinese government's own statement, which has been included in the Basic Law and implemented by the Chinese government in Hong Kong; it has nothing to do with the UK government's right and responsibility. The Chinese side stressed more than once that what policies would be implemented in Hong Kong is China's domestic affairs and need no permission or supervision from any other country. The Chinese government has also reiterated many times over the years that the UK does not have sovereign rule, governing power or supervisory power over Hong Kong affairs, which are China's internal affairs.

The *Joint Declaration* is not the source of legitimacy of the Basic Law, neither is it the legal basis of the Basic Law. The statutory basis of the Basic Law is the Constitution of the PRC, of which Article 31 provides the constitutional ground for the establishment of SARs as well as related legislation. The Constitution is the mother of all Chinese laws, including the Basic Law of the HKSAR. Without the Constitution, the Basic Law would not have been created. The 12 principles and policies the Chinese government put in the *Joint Declaration* were intended to expound the fundamental principles and policies of "one country, two systems", rather than to authorize the legislation of the Basic Law, which was promulgated in accordance with the Constitution of the PRC, not the *Joint Declaration*. As early as 1981, Ye Jianying, Chairman of the NPC Standing Committee officially put forward the central government's nine-point proposal for bringing about the peaceful reunification of the mainland and Taiwan, which outlines the fundamental principles of "one country, two systems".

The Constitution is the ultimate embodiment of sovereignty. There is only one constitution in China. The Basic Law is a constitutional document of the HKSAR; that it is called "Hong

Kong's mini-constitution" is merely a figurative description. Hong Kong must follow not only the Basic Law but also the Constitution. It does not mean that all articles of the Constitution directly apply to Hong Kong, but rather that Hong Kong, as a special administrative region of China, must respect and uphold the country's social system and governance system. Meanwhile, the articles of the Constitution that establish the sovereign powers of "one country" directly apply to the HKSAR. For instance, the Constitution stipulates that Taiwan is a part of China, and the reunification of the Chinese nation is a sacred duty of all Chinese people, including Hong Kong society, of course.

"One country, two systems" is unprecedented, which is why it went through an arduous process of reinvention from a policy concept into a legal system through the implementation of the Basic Law. It began with a drafting committee composed of experts from both the mainland and Hong Kong, which spent four years and eight months to complete the draft Basic Law after two rounds of public consultation over every detail. Figuratively speaking, the Basic Law can be likened to a sword fabricated in ten years. Deng Xiaoping described it as "a law of historic and international significance", as well as "a creative masterpiece". The Basic Law took effect on July 1, 1997, but was promulgated on April 4, 1990. It allowed Hong Kong residents to see how "one country, two systems" would benefit them seven years in advance and thus eased many people's worries about the city's future. It has provided "one country, two systems" with the indispensable legal protection.

Why does "one country, two systems" signify "big changes"?

"Horse racing and stock trading all remain open and robust." That is a popular and vivid depiction of Hong Kong after China resumed the exercise of sovereignty over the city. Indeed, many people interpret "one country, two systems" as "nothing changes". However, this understanding is far too superficial than what the reality is. Deng Xiaoping once said, "One country, two systems" is a "big change". Indeed, since the day of the reunification, Hong Kong has been changing in many ways even though most of its fundamental "original traits" have not.

Make no mistake, the Basic Law stipulates, "The capitalist system and way of life shall remain unchanged for 50 years." Hong Kong is still a free port and a separate customs zone. The city's own currency remains in circulation and English is still an official language along with Chinese. These unique characteristics that define Hong Kong have all been preserved.

However, from a different perspective, we can see for sure Hong Kong's constitutional basis has completely changed. Under British rule, Hong Kong's constitutional document were Hong Kong Letters Patent, and Hong Kong Royal Instructions, which established the foundation of the colonial rule. Hong Kong was regarded as an "overseas territory" by Britain and its public officers had to pledge allegiance to the British Crown. Since its return to the motherland, Hong Kong has become a special administrative region of the PRC, whose Constitution and the Basic Law of the HKSAR together form the constitutional basis of the city; and the public servants swear to uphold the Basic Law and pledge allegiance to the HKSAR. On this new constitutional basis, a custom-made set of governance system and related institutions have been adopted, which help keep the city's characteristics and advantages. In other words, the biggest change is its constitutional basis, which allows other "original traits" to remain unchanged and stable.

The rule of law is the foundation of a functioning society. Hong Kong has maintained its capitalist system and way of life since July 1, 1997, with its existing laws and bylaws largely unchanged. The reason why they are "largely unchanged" instead of "entirely unchanged" is not only because of the introduction of the Basic Law, but also because all existing laws and bylaws must shed everything that was in conflict with the Basic Law for the sake of their constitutional integrity. Before Hong Kong's reunification with the motherland, in accordance with Article 160 of the Basic Law, the NPC Standing Committee spent five years reviewing all the existing laws and bylaws of Hong Kong and took out every bit that was in conflict with the Basic Law. As it turned out, the national legislature decided that Hong Kong's existing statutory infrastructure did not require a major overhaul, and the majority of the legislation should remain effective after all references to "Her Majesty the Queen" and other royal trimmings were replaced with adaptations to reflect the constitutional relationship between the HKSAR and the Central People's Government.

The national Constitution is the constitutional basis for the establishment of special administrative regions, which is unique to China. The Basic Law of the HKSAR was enacted in accordance with Article 31 of the Constitution. The Basic Law establishes the "one country, two systems" principle as the framework of the statutory and institutional system of the SAR; it therefore enjoys supremacy over all existing laws in Hong Kong. It sets in stone, so to speak, the relationship between the central government and the HKSAR, the composition and functions of the HKSAR government as well as the rights and obligations of Hong Kong citizens. It is safe to say the difference between the Basic Law and the British Hong Kong constitutional order is heaven and earth.

Deng Xiaoping once said, "We should not be afraid of changes; any changes are for the betterment of Hong Kong and the maintenance of its prosperity and development, rather than harming the interests of Hong Kong residents." Indeed, Hong Kong has been experiencing changes in the past 25 years, although its capitalist system and way of life have not. Whereas Hong Kong government officials followed orders from London in the past, the SAR government today makes its own decisions, which is what "Hong Kong people governing Hong Kong" means. All the governors of yesteryear were appointed by the British monarch; whereas today the chief executive of the HKSAR is elected by an election committee comprising Hong Kong residents and then appointed by the central government. Under British rule, members of the LegCo were mostly handpicked by the governor, who also chaired LegCo. Today, lawmakers are elected, who in turn elect the president of LegCo among themselves. The right of final adjudication used to rest with the Privy Council in London; but now it is in the hands of the Court of Final Appeal of the HKSAR and signifies an unprecedented level of independent judicial power and final adjudication. Elections in Hong Kong are becoming more and more democratic; Hong Kong deputies to the

NPC and Hong Kong members of the CPPCC directly participate in the administration and deliberation of state affairs.

A significant symbol of the change in the constitutional basis is Hong Kong's reintegration into the national governance system. The brand-new constitutional basis requires Hong Kong citizens to adapt to the new constitutional order, as well as to keep perfecting the systems and mechanisms for the implementation of the Constitution and the Basic Law in the HKSAR. It is crucial to enhance the knowledge of the nation's Constitution and the Basic Law in Hong Kong society, especially among public officials, civil servants and younger generations.

Why can "one country, two systems" be maintained for a long time?

The "one country, two systems" formula of governance must be maintained over the long term. "There is no reason to change it at all", which has proved to be "a good system", President Xi Jinping declared at the 25th anniversary celebration for Hong Kong's return to the motherland. This is no doubt a reaffirmation of the "50 years no change, and no need to change after 50 years" mantra recited by Deng Xiaoping. So what is the rationale behind the notion that "one country, two systems" can be maintained and implemented for a long time?

To answer this question we need to know the premises for keeping "one country, two systems" unchanged for 50 years, as indicated by Deng Xiaoping back then, and whether these preconditions have changed now.

When Deng put forward the idea of "unchanged for 50 years", he emphasized two premises: "Two things will remain unchanged." He said Hong Kong can "keep its capitalist system and way of life unchanged for 50 years or beyond only if the mainland keeps its socialist system unchanged". That means Hong Kong's system will remain unchanged as long as the mainland's remains unchanged. Another precondition is that the country will achieve his "three-step development strategy", which aims to build the country into a moderately developed nation by the middle of the 21st century, not far from the end of "unchanged for 50 years". By then the main body of the country would have become much stronger and more capable of ensuring regional stability than today. Why would anyone want to change the system then? What Deng did not foresee back then is that China would achieve an economic miracle by virtue of reform and opening up that would exceed his expectations by so much as to have achieved the "three-step development strategy" ahead of schedule. That is why the CPC adjusted the strategic development goal at its 19th National Congress in October 2017 and now aims to turn China into a great modernized socialist country by the middle of this century.

To this day, not only have those two premises remained unchanged but become more solid. Deng's and Xi's confidence in "one country, two systems" reflects their faith in socialism with Chinese characteristics as well as their confidence in the great rejuvenation of the Chinese nation. While Deng talked about "no change" based on foresight, Xi talked about "no change" based on solid experience gained from 25 years of practice that has proved "one country, two systems" is an effective governance model with strong adaptability. The central government has made "one country, two systems" part of the fundamental strategy in national governance and handling State affairs; there is no doubt it will uphold the policy unswervingly for a long time.

As such, the real question is with Hong Kong itself. The "black-clad insurrection" that flagrantly promoted "Hong Kong independence" a couple of years ago has made many people worried about the sustainability of "one country, two systems" after 2047. There is reason to be worried and alerted as some disruptive forces inside and outside Hong Kong are hell-bent to derail "one country, two systems". Only when the policy is implemented fully and faithfully without being bent or distorted can its sustainability beyond 2047 be secured.

It may be too early to talk about 2047. But when we consider whether or not to keep Hong Kong's current system, we may refer to a precondition written in the preamble of the Basic Law — the history and realities of Hong Kong. Prior to Hong Kong's return to the motherland, the decision to implement "one country, two systems" and keep it "unchanged for 50 years" was based on the city's history and realities. Therefore, the same logic is applicable when we look beyond 2047. By 2047, if the Basic Law is implemented in an effective way, the "two systems" maintains a harmonious and complementary relationship and the country, including Hong Kong, remains prosperous and stable, it is of course in the best interest of all parties concerned that "one country, two systems" is here to stay.

Although "no change for 50 years" enshrined in the Basic Law should be read literally, it may be seen as another way of saying "unchanged for a long time". Deng Xiaoping once explained, "50 years is just figurative speech, meaning ('one country, two systems') would remain unchanged beyond 50 years." He added that "in the first 50 years, it must not be changed; but after that, it would not be necessary to change." We sincerely hope his prediction will come true.

Why do people say genuine democracy started only after the return?

After Hong Kong's return in 1997, the average Hong Kong resident's right to participate in political affairs has increased far more than it has had at any point under British rule. Those who accuse the central authorities of dragging their feet over Hong Kong's democratic development are clearly unfair, as they offer nothing to compare historically and obviously do not understand the relevant principles enshrined in the Basic Law.

In November 2021, the State Council Information Office issued a white paper, titled "Hong Kong: Democratic Progress Under the Framework of 'One Country, Two Systems'". The white paper gives a detailed and systematic historical account of Hong Kong's democratic development, reaffirms the central government's firm support for Hong Kong's democratic development, and further elucidates the central government's principles and stance on Hong Kong's democratic development.

Britain maintained colonial rule over Hong Kong, which has been described as a "living fossil of early imperial politics". From the time of British occupation till the 1960s, political powers were tightly held in the hands of the governors and British nationals in public offices, while ethnic Chinese residents who accounted for 98% of the population had almost no right to participate in political affairs, except that a few individuals were co-opted into the Executive Council and Legislative Council for the purpose of displaying "political openness". The UK government expressly excluded the provision on periodic elections when it ratified the *International Covenant on Civil and Political Rights* for implementation in Hong Kong 1976. A former British principal official in Hong Kong who retired in 1981 once said in a public speech that throughout his 30-year tenure, "democracy" was always a dirty word. This is because the British Hong Kong government firmly believed that, once introduced into the city, democracy would destroy the local economy and cause sociopolitical instability surely in no time. When democracy was experimented with for the very first time in the District Council elections of 1982, the British Hong Kong government boasted that it was "the first successful step in the early stage of civic participation in Hong Kong politics". By that time it was already universally known that China would take back Hong Kong. When some people won the LegCo election in 1991 by direct vote in geographical constituencies for the first time in history, the Basic Law of the HKSAR has already been promulgated by the NPC.

The late Prime Minister Margaret Thatcher wrote in her memoir that she knew, while Sino-British negotiations over Hong Kong were still going on, that it would be impossible for the UK to continue governing the city, and therefore decided back then to develop a democratic framework to facilitate a speedy process for Hong Kong to gain independence or complete autonomy. To this end, the British Hong Kong government produced a series of white papers on representative politics from the 1980s and introduced elections in a hasty manner over the following years. This well-calculated political reform process culminated in the last governor Christopher Patten's radical reforms, which would not have been launched were the British continued to rule over Hong Kong. The "path dependence" created by those radical political reforms has violated the principles established by the Basic Law, setting up traps for the future special administrative region.

Hong Kong opened a new era of institutionalized democratic development after its return to the motherland, with "Hong Kong people governing Hong Kong" being the strongest feature of its democracy as it put an end to the British's control of all power in the executive and legislative branches as well as the final adjudication. The SAR government and the LegCo are comprised of locals; both the number of the Election Committee and that of directly-elected seats in the LegCo have been increased gradually; and "dual universal suffrage" would have been implemented for the 2017 Chief Executive Election and the 2020 LegCo Election had the opposition not rejected the electoral reform package proposed by the government.

It is never a good idea to pursue electoral reform in total disregard of social condition. The Basic Law stipulates in Articles 45 and 68 that the methods for the selection of the chief executive and legislators "shall be specified in the light of the actual situation in the Hong Kong Special Administrative Region and in accordance with the principle of gradual and orderly progress". There is no disagreement among all parties concerned on the goal of electoral reform in Hong Kong. Differences have always been in how soon the goal is to be achieved — in a rush or an orderly fashion. In other words, the difference is between promoting democracy based on an abstract term or in accordance with Hong Kong's real conditions. From direct election to universal suffrage, it took France 140 years, the United States 170 years, and the UK 560 years. Hasty implementation of universal suffrage without taking into consideration the actual social conditions would inevitably bring about social split-up and chaos that would ultimately wreak havoc on the economy and rule of law.

Why has "dual universal suffrage" not been achieved in the SAR?

Unfortunately, the door to "dual universal suffrage" was shut by the "pan-democratic" lawmakers, who on June 18, 2015 vetoed the electoral reform package for the implementation of universal suffrage for the 2017 Chief Executive Election drafted and proposed by the HKSAR government based on the NPCSC's decision issued on August 31, 2014 (the "8.31 decision").

This was not the first time the "pan-democratic" lawmakers blocked electoral reform. They already vetoed in 2005 another electoral reform package aimed at making the electoral process more democratic. They have since been dubbed by angry Hong Kong residents as the "opposition camp".

There is no mentioning of universal suffrage in the *Sino-British Joint Declaration*. It is the Basic Law that sets the goal of implementing "dual universal suffrage", therefore the Chinese government is the designer and steadfast promoter of democratic institutions for the special administrative region. Article 45 reads: "The ultimate aim is the selection of the Chief Executive by universal suffrage after nomination by a broadly representative nominating committee in accordance with democratic procedures." Article 68 says: "The ultimate aim is the election of all the members of the Legislative Council by universal suffrage." On Dec 29, 2007, the NPCSC reached a decision that set the timetable for implementing "dual universal suffrage" for the chief executive in 2017 and for the LegCo later (12.29 decision). The "8.31 decision" supplements the "12.29 decision" by adopting specific rules over the election of the chief executive via universal suffrage. "Dual universal suffrage" would have been realized had the "pan-democratic" lawmakers not vetoed the electoral reform package in 2015.

The opposition lawmakers claimed that the 2015 electoral reform package, which includes a "candidate screening mechanism", is not one for "genuine universal suffrage", and demanded the withdrawal of the "8.31 decision". They also demanded modifications in the screening mechanism, including the addition of "civil nomination" and "party nomination" — a move aimed at encroaching on the Nominating Committee's exclusive power and thus violates the Basic Law. Another modification they asked for was to lower the requirement of obtaining the support of more than half of the Nominating Committee members for a candidate to be qualified to run in the chief executive election. That the opposition camp was opposed to even the rule of majority — a universal democratic principle — suggested that they merely fretted over the gloomy prospect of their candidates joining the race.

Is it justifiable to have a screening mechanism? To answer this question, one needs to understand the relationship between "one country" and "two systems" as well as the principle of "patriots administering Hong Kong". The requirement of "institutional nomination" by the Nominating Committee as stipulated by the Basic Law and the requirement of support by more than half of the Nominating Committee members as required by the "8.31 decision" are intended to help screen out candidates who antagonize the central government, and who eventually would harm national security and Hong Kong's interests — by means of the wisdom of majority. "Hong Kong people governing Hong Kong" means the administration of Hong Kong affairs by patriots; the chief executive being the ultimate embodiment of "Hong Kong people governing Hong Kong" must be a patriot. The "8.31 decision" emphasizes that "this is the basic requirement of 'one country, two systems', and that the method for the selection of the chief executive via universal suffrage must provide institutional safeguards for this requirement".

Admittedly, nomination is a screening process. In the United States, the presidential candidates are nominated by the two dominant parties, and in the United Kingdom, the prime minister is nominated by the ruling party; both are a form of screening. The chief executive of the HKSAR is accountable to both the SAR and the central government. The role of the chief executive is so crucial to the successful implementation of "one country, two systems" that all candidates are rightly required to pass the nomination process to ensure that only candidates with both majority support and the trust of the central government are able to enter the race. Moreover, the chief executive-elect will need to be appointed by the central government. Clearly, there can be no compromise when it comes to the "8.31 decision".

The white paper, titled "Hong Kong: Democratic Progress Under the Framework of One Country, Two Systems", hits home when it notes that "the key issue that has emerged in the course of developing democracy in Hong Kong over the past two decades is not whether Hong Kong should pursue democracy. Rather, it is an issue of upholding the 'One Country' principle".

Why should a democratic electoral system with Hong Kong characteristics be built?

The opposition camp in Hong Kong betted everything on achieving "dual universal suffrage" immediately by resorting to all means imaginable and blamed all the problems Hong Kong has on the absence of "one person one vote". But the model they insisted on is way off the kind of electoral system that should be adopted under the "one country, two systems" policy.

Deng Xiaoping, when discussing the electoral system for Hong Kong back in the day, said, "There exists the assertion that universal suffrage suits Hong Kong no matter what. I don't believe." "Those who administer Hong Kong should be Hong Kong people who love the motherland and Hong Kong equally. But can anyone guarantee universal suffrage alone will return such administrators?" "Even if universal suffrage is to be held, it must be implemented in a gradual manner." "If Hong Kong copies the Western model no matter what, it will suffer a lot when social unrest happens."

There is no international standard for an electoral system. For example, those of the United States and United Kingdom are different. Some people insist on taking "universal and equal suffrage", which is mentioned in Article 25 of the *International Covenant on Civil and Political Rights*, as the international standard for democratic elections. They could have easily hoodwinked people with their dazzling banners or slogans. The fact is, Article 25 of the *International Covenant* merely lists three principles without specifying any methods of election. The United Nations published in 1994 a handbook on the basic international human rights principles relating to elections, which is titled "Human Rights and Elections: A Handbook on the Legal, Technical and Human Rights Aspects of Elections". In that handbook, the UN human rights body states that there is no political system or electoral method that works for all people or all countries, and it objects to any attempt to impose an existing political model on any society.

The most important criterion in rating electoral systems is whether it suits a particular country or region the best. The best way to know if a shoe fits is to wear it. The criteria for evaluating Hong Kong's electoral system are not the existing models of Western countries but two specific conditions. The first is its constitutional order. Hong Kong is a special administrative region of a unitary state, and its elections are regional events that must be designed with the relationship between the SAR and the central government as well as national interest and security in mind. That means it cannot be modeled after the electoral systems of sovereign states. The other one is Hong Kong's actual situation. That means Hong Kong's constitutional development must proceed in a gradual and orderly fashion according to the Basic Law, let the democratic process evolve harmoniously with its social development as the actual situation permits, and proceed in accordance with the law and in an orderly manner, preventing a harmful rush to extreme democracy. The HKSAR's electoral system should facilitate balanced participation by all sectors of society, so as to benefit economic development and social stability. It must help enhance executive-legislative relations, strengthen the executive-led administration as stipulated by the Basic Law, and achieve good governance.

By the way, "progress in an orderly fashion" was first raised by David Wilson, who was governor of Hong Kong from April 9, 1987, to July 3, 1992. That idea won the support of late Chinese leader Deng Xiaoping and was eventually written into the Basic Law of the HKSAR.

There is no single set of criteria for democracy and no single model of democracy that is universally acceptable. Democracy comes in many forms. It cannot be reduced to the simplistic question of whether there are elections, and elections themselves cannot be defined exclusively as direct elections. The overall interests and common aspirations of society can be better served by expanding multiple democratic processes such as public consultation and inquiry, as well as pursuing high-quality whole-process democracy that put emphasis on both the election and governance processes. Political reforms are intended for achieving good governance, rather than merely "one person, one vote". That many governments in the West are mired in election politics and vetocracy, and thus becoming increasingly ineffective is a subject that deserves the attention of Hong Kong people.

The Basic Law of the HKSAR not only sets the ultimate goal of achieving universal suffrage in both the chief executive and LegCo elections, following a gradual and orderly process, but also establishes the constitutional order of Hong Kong and stipulates the conditions for universal suffrage. It is unacceptable to justify the ultimate goal of electoral reform with the Basic Law but discuss methods of election without referring to the Basic Law. The improvement of the HKSAR's electoral system in 2021 is a reconstruction and optimization of the existing system that is in line with the current stage of democratic development in Hong

Kong. As it progresses toward universal suffrage, the HKSAR must always stick to "one country, two systems" in pursuit of democracy with Hong Kong characteristics. Ultimately, Hong Kong must adhere to the Constitution and the Basic Law when promoting democracy.

Why did the central authorities enact the National Security Law for Hong Kong?

The Standing Committee of the National People's Congress passed the Law of the People's Republic of China on Safeguarding National Security in the Hong Kong Special Administrative Region on June 30, 2020. It put an end to the absence of national security protection in Hong Kong. Why did the NPCSC still need to enact such a law for Hong Kong even though Article 23 of the Basic Law has already authorized the HKSAR to legislate to safeguard national security?

The Hong Kong National Security Law is a law that was long overdue. National security is the core of national sovereignty; all relevant legislation and enforcement actions should naturally be carried out by the central authorities. Nonetheless, the central authorities have authorized the HKSAR to enact such a law as stipulated in Article 23 of the Basic Law under the "one country, two systems" framework after taking into consideration the differences in between the legal systems of the Chinese mainland and Hong Kong. Such a special arrangement also reflects the central authorities' high trust in the HKSAR. Unfortunately, the HKSAR has failed to legislate according to Article 23. The absence of a law for Hong Kong to fulfill its constitutional obligation in protecting national security allowed separatist forces to advocate "Hong Kong independence" in recent years and launch a "color revolution" known as "black revolution" in Hong Kong in 2019, when "black-clad" rioters or anti-China subversives, raised hell in Hong Kong in collusion with hostile external forces with the most destructive unrest since the city returned to the motherland in 1997. This posed a direct threat to China's national security as well as the safety of the HKSAR government, forcing the central authorities to take action and end the dangerous situation in Hong Kong. The central authorities are authorized by the Constitution to retain the power and assume the ultimate responsibility of protecting national security, which shall not be affected by Article 23 of the Basic Law of the HKSAR. Nothing can stop the central authorities from pushing for national security legislation for the HKSAR when the latter is not in a position to fulfill its constitutional obligation to safeguard national security by legislating according to Article 23 of the Basic Law.

Development cannot proceed without security. The National

Security Law for Hong Kong is designed solely to protect the country's national security and ensure the security of the HKSAR government. It prevents, stops, and punishes crimes of secession, subversion of state power, terrorist activities, and colluding with external forces to endanger national security, all of which are posted a grave threat to national security in recent years, especially during the anti-extradition bill campaign. The National Security Law enforced in Hong Kong only targets a small number of criminals while protecting the freedom of speech and other rights of Hong Kong residents recognized by the Basic Law.

To address the absence of a law in Hong Kong to fulfill its national security obligations and the HKSAR authority's inability to stop such harmful behavior in the region, the National Security Law promulgated for the HKSAR names four crimes for severe punishment upon conviction, with enforcement mechanisms to boot, including setting up the Committee for Safeguarding National Security of the HKSAR, appointing a national security adviser to the committee by the central government, establishing a national security division in the Hong Kong Police Force and an office in charge of prosecuting national security crimes in the Department of Justice, along with requiring the chief executive of the HKSAR to designate judges to handle national security cases along with to file national security reports to the central authorities regularly. Another key national security law enforcement measure is the establishment of the Office for Safeguarding National Security of the Central People's Government in the HKSAR to supervise, guide, coordinate and support the HKSAR in fulfilling its constitutional responsibilities for safeguarding national security. The HKSAR maintains jurisdiction over all national security-related criminal cases occurring in Hong Kong except the three types listed in Article 55 of the National Security Law, which shall be handled by the Office for Safeguarding National Security of the Central People's Government in the HKSAR and the mainland law enforcement departments concerned according to relevant national laws. The establishment of two national security law enforcement mechanisms on state and regional levels is a significant innovation in the exercise of "one country, two systems".

The National Security Law enforced in Hong Kong does not exempt the HKSAR from fulfilling its constitutional obligation to legislate according to Article 23 of the Basic Law; it does not cover all seven crimes against national security listed in Article 23. That means the HKSAR must assume its constitutional responsibility in safeguarding national security by completing its own legislation according to Article 23 of the Basic Law as soon as possible, as stipulated in Article 7 of the National

Security Law. A tailor-made national security law, instead of the National Security Law of the People's Republic of China, is implemented in Hong Kong; the HKSAR handles the vast majority of its national security cases; and the National Security Law for Hong Kong does not exempt the HKSAR from fulfilling its constitutional obligation to legislate according to Article 23 of the Basic Law. All of these arrangements have been adopted after taking into consideration the actual situation in Hong Kong and reflect the principle of "one country, two systems".

"One country" is the host of "two systems", meaning the "one country, two systems" principle works only when the country's national security is intact. President Xi Jinping has laid down "three bottom lines" for "one country, two systems" that must never be crossed, and the National Security Law enforced in Hong Kong is the institutional embodiment of the "three bottom lines".

Why can't Article 23 legislation be further delayed?

It has been more than 20 years since Hong Kong returned to the motherland, but the SAR has yet to fulfill its constitutional obligation of enacting national security legislation according to Article 23 of the Basic Law. Because of this delay, Hong Kong had remained a national security liability before the National Security Law for Hong Kong was promulgated.

The central government put Hong Kong in a special position by blessing it with the "one country, two systems" principle because it is conducive to achieving and upholding national unification. Article 23 of the Basic Law stipulates that the HKSAR shall enact laws on its own to prohibit seven types of activities harmful to national security. It is more an instruction than an authorization for Hong Kong to enact a local-version national security law. The National Security Law of the People's Republic of China promulgated in 2015 clearly requires the HKSAR and Macao SAR to fulfill their responsibilities in safeguarding national security. As a Chinese saying goes, "hair dies without skin." The existence of "two systems" does not spare the SAR from its obligation to safeguard national security. And there is no point talking about "two systems" when "one country" is in danger.

Some people have called for completing national security legislation according to Article 23 of the Basic Law before implementing "dual universal suffrage" in Hong Kong. That makes sense since "dual universal suffrage" could pose a political threat in the absence of a law safeguarding national security from Hong Kong's end. However, the central government has not tied the two together, and the NPC announced in 2007 a timetable for implementing "dual universal suffrage" in Hong Kong. This is yet another example of the central government's confidence in the people of Hong Kong. The truth is that national security legislation according to Article 23 of the Basic Law must be fulfilled with or without "dual universal suffrage". The HKSAR cannot choose not to honor this constitutional obligation.

The HKSAR has the constitutional and principal responsibility of safeguarding national security. It has been 20 years since the HKSAR government's first attempt to enact a national security law according to Article 23 failed in 2003. Hong

Kong's existing laws also contain provisions related to national security. However, these existing laws are not enough to replace a national security law tailor-made to meet the requirements of Article 23 of the Basic Law; and they have been dormant for a long time for various reasons. As a result of the long delay in legislation according to Article 23, "Hong Kong independence" advocacy has risen over recent years; while a host of political groups and figures have been busy conspiring with hostile forces overseas to gravely threaten national security as well as jeopardizing the safety of the HKSAR government over recent years, highlighting the huge hidden danger posed by the absence of a legislation according to Article 23. The 19th CPC Central Committee adopted a decision at its fourth plenary session on October 31, requiring the enactment and improvement of national security laws and related enforcement mechanisms in the two SARs amid a raging insurrection staged by the "black-clad" rioters in Hong Kong. The enactment of the National Security Law by the central authorities for enforcement in Hong Kong timely filled the legal vacuum, promptly put an end to violence and restored social order, facilitating the city's transition from chaos to good governance. It is also a warning to the SAR that the Article 23 legislation can't be delayed any longer.

Both the National Security Law for Hong Kong and Article

23 legislation are crucial to the HKSAR safeguarding national security; they are not a replacement for each other. Article 23 legislation can complement the National Security Law for Hong Kong by covering those areas that are not included in the latter, strengthening the defense of national security.

Fears that Article 23 legislation will erode human rights are unwarranted because national security legislation only targets criminal acts. Moreover, no international conventions or laws on human rights ever suggest that human rights and freedoms shall override national security and public order.

When some people suggested back in the day that China may not need to maintain a military presence in Hong Kong, the then-State leader Deng Xiaoping responded rather angrily and emphasized that a military presence is a symbol of sovereignty and a means to preventing "things that will harm the country's fundamental interests" from happening. Deng's wisdom and foresight were undeniable in terms of "expecting the worst". He decided that, "should social unrest occur (in Hong Kong), the central government must step in", when necessary, the People's Liberation Army Hong Kong Garrison may also lend a hand in stopping violent unrest. Some people are worried that dispatching PLA troops would signify the end of "one country, two systems". Such concern is unwarranted. Article 14 of the

Basic Law stipulates: "The Government of the Hong Kong Special Administrative Region may, when necessary, ask the Central People's Government for assistance from the garrison in the maintenance of public order and in disaster relief." Quelling social unrest is the responsibility of the garrison just as national defense is.

Why has Beijing adopted a "winning combo" of National Security Law and electoral revamp for Hong Kong?

The National People's Congress adopted, in May 2020, a decision on establishing and improving the legal system and enforcement mechanisms for the HKSAR to safeguard national security. In accordance with the NPC decision, its Standing Committee proceeded to promulgate the National Security Law for Hong Kong, which took effect on June 30, 2020. In March 2021, the NPC passed another decision on improving the electoral system of the HKSAR and authorized its Standing Committee to amend Annex I and Annex II to the Basic Law, so that the HKSAR could implement the electoral reform through local legislation. The two statutory milestones have been so effective that they are now widely hailed in Hong Kong as well as around the world as a "winning combo".

The main challenges facing the HKSAR since its

establishment in July 1997 can be summed up by two problems. One was its inability to maintain stability due to constant sabotage by local anti-China subversive forces colluding with hostile external forces, which posed grave threats to national security of the country as well as Hong Kong's stability. The other was the HKSAR government's inability to administer the region effectively, mainly because of dogged obstruction by local opposition parties who indiscriminately politicized all major issues and relentlessly filibustered in the LegCo. Those problems caused the ultimate damage to Hong Kong during the "black revolution" (June 2019-June 2020), when the "black-clad" rioters pushed the city to the brink of total chaos. If the problems were not solved in a timely manner, it would have led the practice of "one country, two systems" to a complete failure. Since the HKSAR government did not have the political prowess to head off those problems immediately, the central authorities had to take matters into their hands according to the nation's Constitution and the Basic Law of the HKSAR. Before Hong Kong's return to the motherland, the NPC adopted eight decisions regarding the question of Hong Kong, but only two in the more than two decades since its return. That alone says a lot about the political impact of the "winning combo".

As it turns out, the National Security Law for Hong

Kong ended violent riots in the city immediately, allowing it to restore peace and order; while the improved electoral system has effectively prevented the anti-China subversive forces from infiltrating the governance structure of the HKSAR as they did through the old, flawed electoral system. As a result, the HKSAR government has been able to do its job much more smoothly and effectively, laying the ground for solving the city's deep-seated problems as well as consolidating the institutional foundation for the smooth implementation of "one country, two systems" in the long run.

The "winning combo" is a mechanism to uphold the original intent of "one country, two systems". When Deng Xiaoping put forward the monumental system arrangement, for Hong Kong after its return to the motherland, he also spelled out some preconditions, the most important of which was that the territorial integrity and the social system of the main body of the country must not change, because "that would end Hong Kong's prosperity and stability as well". Another crucial precondition was "patriots administering Hong Kong", because otherwise "the people of Hong Kong administer Hong Kong" principle would lose its soul. The enactment of the National Security law for Hong Kong and the improvement of the city's electoral system help uphold the original intent of "one country, two systems" by rebuilding the SAR's political order and political ethics.

The "winning combo" is also an improvement to the mechanism of implementing "one country, two systems" in Hong Kong. The Basic Law leaves two "assignments" for the HKSAR to fulfill. One is Article 23, which requires Hong Kong to complete national security legislation outlawing seven types of acts that endanger national security within Hong Kong's jurisdiction. The other is the optimization of the local electoral system, for achieving universal suffrage ultimately in Hong Kong in accordance with the actual situation and in a gradual manner after its return to China. Unfortunately, Article 23 legislation had yet to be fulfilled more than two decades after Hong Kong's return; leaving national security and HKSAR's governance at risk; and the old, flawed electoral system afforded anti-China subversive forces the chance to seize the governing power of the HKSAR. The promulgation of the National Security Law for Hong Kong and the improvement of its electoral system have complemented the Basic Law in a significant way by plugging an institutional loophole.

The "winning combo" highlights governance according to the law in Hong Kong. The central government has emphasized repeatedly the need to improve the system and mechanisms of implementing "one country, two systems" according to the Basic

Law as well as the Constitution. The construction and continuous improvement of laws and their enforcement mechanisms are fundamental means to consistently improve the governance of the HKSAR. It is more effective to tackle problems through the designated system and its related enforcement mechanisms than through any other means.

Hong Kong society has long been confused by two myths: One has crippled national awareness by upsetting the relationship between "one country" and "two systems", in some cases to total disregard of the nation's sovereignty, national security and development interest; while the other has turned the concept of democracy on its head by advocating Western-style representative democracy with religious-like ardent zest without considering Hong Kong's constitutional order which sets boundaries for its democratic development. With the "winning combo", the central authorities have spelled out Hong Kong's constitutional obligation to safeguard national security, defined the framework for a democratic system consistent with Hong Kong's reality and helped break Hong Kong society out of the myths.

Why is "one country, two systems" so inclusive?

Last century witnessed fierce confrontations between capitalist and socialist blocs. The sheer differences between the two social systems are easy to see. As such it requires great political confidence and strong sense of inclusiveness to let these different social systems coexist in one country harmoniously and as mutually benefiting as possible.

This bold and creative institutional arrangement is rooted in Chinese culture and wisdom, which favors diversity in unity, just like rivers emptying into the ocean with no concerns of overflowing. In Hong Kong the goal is to build the broadest consensus among socio-political groups with major rather than minor differences, because the central government is confident that the differences between Hong Kong and the mainland can and that will be harmonized through peaceful fine-tuning under "one country, two systems". Late Chinese leader Deng Xiaoping once said that as long as they contribute to national unity regardless of ethnicity, "all political opinions should be tolerated, including those opposed to the Communist Party of China". More recently, President Xi Jinping summarized the expansiveness and inclusiveness of "one country, two systems" as "enhancing the development of the mainland, which exercises socialism with Chinese characteristics, as well as that of Hong Kong, which remains a capitalist society".

Hong Kong's high degree of autonomy dwarfs that of the states in confederate democracies in the West. Since July 1, 1997 Hong Kong has remained a free port and separate customs territory with its own finance, tax and currency systems as well as the common law-based judicial system. It is absolutely unique in that it does not pay any tax to the State or bear the expenses of the People's Liberation Army Hong Kong Garrison, the military expenditures of the British troops stationed in Hong Kong were paid for by the Hong Kong people. Hong Kong today also enjoys judicial independence, including the power of final adjudication, which belonged to Her Majesty's Most Honorable Privy Council in London before China resumed the exercise of sovereignty over Hong Kong. Final adjudication is a power reserved for the sovereign state and is not available to the local authorities in most, if not all, countries, for fear that the country's political stability is undermined by the disunity in the interpretation of law. The Basic Law grants Hong Kong the power of final adjudication after taking into consideration Hong Kong's actual situation—the practice of the common law system in the city. This arrangement is a breakthrough in the conventional governance model.

In addition to authorizing Hong Kong to exercise high-degree autonomy, the central government also treats Hong Kong residents with phenomenal trust. When the HKSAR was established, 21 of the 23 principal officials serving in the British-Hong Kong government, except one foreign national who was banned by the Basic Law to serve in the HKSAR government and another one who was ready to retire and therefore replaced, were appointed by the central government to service in the SAR government. All the civil servants hired by the British-Hong Kong government, believed to top 180,000 at that time, were able to keep their jobs in the SAR government. The central government does not interfere in what is deemed the internal affairs of the HKSAR according to the Basic Law. In fact, the HKSAR is represented in the National People's Congress, the highest organ of State power, and the political advisory body, the Chinese People's Political Consultative Conference. Civil servants in the HKSAR government have been chosen to work in international agencies, such as the United Nations, as members of Chinese delegations. Even in crucial matters such as national security, Hong Kong has been trusted with completing its own legislation according to Article 23 of the Basic Law, which could have been done by the NPC Standing Committee instead.

The central government's Hong Kong policies can be seen as serving two general purposes — "containment" and "induction". "Containment" refers to the "three bottom lines" that absolutely forbid any attempt to endanger national sovereignty and security, challenge the power of the central government and the authority of the Basic Law of the HKSAR or use Hong Kong to carry out infiltration and sabotage activities against the mainland. Such bans are imperative to ensure "one country" at all times. "Induction" means encouraging the HKSAR to integrate its own development into the country's overall development strategy and join the rest of the Chinese nation in pursuing further reform and opening-up as well as the great rejuvenation of the nation. Beneficial measures to this end include the Closer Economic Partnership Arrangement (CEPA), the national five-year plans, the Guangdong–Hong Kong–Macao Greater Bay Area, and all favorable policies and rules designed to help Hong Kong and Macao residents live, work and go to school on the mainland, which offer new opportunities for Hong Kong to further its prosperity and development. While "containment" is rigid, "induction" is inspiring and forward-looking in nature. Between them lies the tremendous space called a high degree of autonomy.

"One country, two systems" as an institutional arrangement is designed to maintain a maximum balance between the best interest of the country and that of Hong Kong society. Philosophically speaking, it demonstrates how "unity of opposites" exists in productive harmony without losing their edges. The "two systems" are inherently at odds with each other but held together by the "greatest common denominator" — "loving the country as a whole and Hong Kong as a particular part of it". With this shared core value at heart, we can achieve greatness despite whatever differences may exist between "two systems".

Conclusion: Strengthening confidence in the institutions of "one country, two systems"

Hong Kong has generally maintained steady development since China resumed the exercise of sovereignty peacefully over the city, more than enough to prove "one country, two systems" is the best solution to the question of Hong Kong left over from history and the best institutional arrangement for the special administrative region to sustain long-term prosperity and stability. Anyone whose heart is in the right place should agree "one country, two systems" is the fruit of brilliant political wisdom and is unmatched in serving its purpose.

"One country, two systems" is an unprecedented, groundbreaking arrangement that must be evaluated in the context of history and the overall situation. First of all, we must distinguish between system and governance. Social systems provide the basic structure for a society to operate, but how effective a system is depends on governance. The root of many problems facing Hong Kong can be traced back to constraints on the executive-led governance, which in turn have undermined the SAR's social management. Also, it is necessary to distinguish the deep-seated problems of Hong Kong society from "one country, two systems". For example, nagging issues such as the short supply of residential housing and the growing wealth gap had long existed before "one country, two systems" came into existence and can only be blamed on the capitalist system alone. The undeniable fact is that Hong Kong was able to prevail over such adversity as the Asia financial crisis of 1997 and the SARS epidemic of 2003 thanks mainly to strong support by the central government and mainland compatriots in accordance with the "one country, two systems" principle. That is why Hong Kong's status as an international financial center, trade hub and shipping center has remained intact for the past 25 years.

In hindsight, had the HKSAR government been able to proceed with the previous plan to build 85,000 housing units every year, would the public housing applicants still have to wait for so many years as they do now? Had the HKSAR government been able to focus more on developing the economy and improving people's livelihoods, instead of having to spend so much energy and public resources on overcoming political obstructions, Hong Kong's socioeconomic development would have been much faster than it actually was over the years. Does anyone believe Hong Kong would still be suffering so much "pain" without all the political infighting and social unrest at the hands of the opposition camp on behalf of the hostile foreign forces and facilitated by the political and institutional traps laid by the British rulers before they left?

Mainstream popular wishes before July 1, 1997 were to maintain the existing capitalist system with more democratic incentives added to the mix going forward. The central authorities were well aware of and understood the public sentiment back then and assured Hong Kong society that its capitalist system and way of life will be unchanged for 50 years by enshrining the promise in the Basic Law of the HKSAR, which also stipulates Hong Kong's electoral reform shall proceed steadily and orderly toward the ultimate goal of universal suffrage in both the chief executive and LegCo elections. Had the HKSAR been able to proceed according to the Basic Law all the time, it would have achieved the goals in time, but the progress was repeatedly interrupted by illegal movements with unconstitutional demands in violation of the Basic Law, plunging local society into endless political dispute and economic hardship. More recently, even separatist advocacy got more rampant, with serious damage to public interests in addition to posing a real threat to national security as well as sovereignty. Such disruptive and costly attempts run against the "one country, two systems" principle and will only push Hong Kong further away from realizing its aspirations.

We can handle the present situation better by drawing lessons from past experiences. Hong Kong cannot solve its problems by going astray from "one country, two systems" or merely by implementing "one person, one vote", but by bringing the advantages of "one country, two systems" as an institutional arrangement into full play by improving the HKSAR's governance, strengthening its growth momentum, resolving people's livelihood problems, and maintaining social harmony and stability under the guidance of the "four aspirations" put forward by President Xi Jinping.

Deng Xiaoping had total confidence in "one country, two systems" back in the day and so do we today. President Xi Jinping has emphasized, "There is no reason to change such a good system and it must be adhered to over the long run." The confidence comes from knowing that the "one country, two systems" principle serves the overall interest of Hong Kong as well as of the nation in the long run and its inclusiveness; from the mind-blowing development of the country toward the "dual centennial goals"; from the orienteering guidance of the Basic Law and the central government's guiding support; and from the fact that "one country, two systems", with its robust adaptability, is capable of coping with the new challenges and problems encountered in practice.

The great rejuvenation of the Chinese nation is an irreversible historical process with the successful implementation of "one country, two systems" in Hong Kong as a vital part of it. Hong Kong will write a new chapter of development under "one country, two systems" for sure by making full use of its advantages afforded by the strong backing of the motherland and the city's strong connectivity with the rest of the world, "undeterred by the occasional hindrances" and "undistracted by the external interferences", as President Xi Jinping has suggested.

As I pointed out in the first article of this series: Remain true to our original aspiration, and one will achieve the ultimate goal in due course.

(Note: All quotes attributed to Deng Xiaoping in this book are from the Chinese book *Deng Xiaoping on Hong Kong issues* published by the Joint Publishing [Hong Kong] Company Limited in November 1993.)

Annex:

Three loaded questions put to young Hong Kong people

Yang Jianping

A few days ago, I was invited to a dinner party organized by the Hong Kong Tianjin Friendship Association (HKTJFA) to celebrate the 70th anniversary of the founding of New China along with the 25th anniversary of the HKTJFA. Signs of positive energy, such as laughter, singing and dancing, permeated the entire venue.

Thanks to my alma mater, Nankai University, I have become attached to the city of Tianjin. I was fortunate enough to be among the first batch of undergraduates who spent an enjoyable four years in Nankai after the National College Entrance Examination was reinstated after the "cultural revolution" (1966-1976). This year not only marks the 70th birthday of New China, but also happens to be the centennial of Nankai University. A ceremonious celebration for my alma mater was held on October 17.

I have regretted not being able to return to Tianjin to attend the celebration. Nonetheless, memories of my alma mater always linger in my mind, with the most striking one being the three questions on patriotism posed by the founding president, Zhang Boling.

"Are you Chinese?"
"Do you love China?"
"Do you wish China well?"

These three thought-provoking questions struck a chord with many people who were struggling to find a solution to the old China's predicament, and sparked the passion and patriotism among students and staff of Nankai University, which has since maintained a tradition of patriotism. When Japan waged war against China, Japanese invaders bombed the campus of Nankai University in an attempt to annihilate the local resistance against Japanese invaders. However, the Nankai community was not intimidated! A large number of Nankai students quit school to join the army and went to the frontline of the war against the Japanese invasion. The third son of the school president Zhang was one of them. He joined the air force and fought the enemy in the sky, eventually sacrificing his young life for the country.

Today, the three questions on patriotism are largely seen on the Nankai campus. At the beginning of the new school year, the president of the school asks each question aloud in front of the teachers and students, who all respond with an affirmative answer. That atmosphere is rousing and breathtaking.

Looking at the current situation of Hong Kong, the "three questions on patriotism" has made me deeply reflective.

President Xi Jinping said, "A nation that forgets its origins will find itself in a blind alley." Many Hong Kong youngsters are oblivious of Chinese contemporary history in which our motherland were subject to foreign aggression and humiliation. They are unfamiliar with the fact that China has undergone earth-shaking reforms since the founding of New China; they are unaware of the inextricable connection between Hong Kong and the motherland in which we share weal and woe together as a single entity, and lack a sense of identity with their own country. Not only is it the bitter fruit of British colonial rule, but also it is the result of a serious deficiency in education since the reunification.

Apart from the deep-seated social and livelihood issues, the current unrest in Hong Kong exposes the reality that some people in Hong Kong, particularly some youngsters, are misinformed about the Chinese mainland. Some of them are so misguided that they are taking advantage of the anti-extradition-bill movement to vent their unwarranted hatred against their own country and even blatantly advocate separatism. This demonstrates how seriously national identity has been distorted in Hong Kong society!

Feeling distressed, I cannot help but raise my own three questions for young people in Hong Kong.

My first question: Do you know the China of today?

As New China enters its 70-year anniversary, it has transformed itself from the "sick man of East Asia" to the second-largest economy in the world, with GDP greater than that of Japan and European Union put together. The life expectancy of the Chinese population has increased from about 30 years to more than 70 years. With a population of 1.4 billion people, China has a comprehensive industrial system, with huge capacity in innovation and national defense, which enables China to play an important role in international affairs. The reform and opening-up policy has facilitated rapid and sustained economic growth over the past 40 years. On average, every three seconds has seen one person climb out of poverty, which is regarded as a miracle by the United Nations. The Beidou Navigation Satellite System, the Jiao Long submarine, the Chang'e robotic spacecraft mission, the 5G technology and the Hong Kong–Zhuhai–Macao Bridge are remarkable technological and infrastructural developments that have showcased the country's progress. In the past 20 years, the increase in forested area in the world is equivalent to an Amazon rainforest — and one-quarter of the new forested area is contributed by China.

Some people might sniff at China's political system while admiring its economic achievements. Indeed, if American-style democracy is regarded as the benchmark, China will probably never pass the test as it does not embrace the multiparty system or the separation of powers. There are also elections in China, but the focus is more on consultation, which better reflects the true meaning of democracy. The executive, legislature, judiciary and supervision are modern governing institutions that China has also established, while the Chinese People's Political Consultative Conference is unique to China. One-party rule, multi-party collaboration and political consultation form a political system that balances fairness and efficiency, which enables the country to concentrate on macro initiatives and reduce political wrangling. This political establishment is more suitable to China's national conditions and better caters to the country's need for rapid development, and it therefore has become a protection mechanism that guarantees New China's economic take-off. Western countries like to label China as "powerful in economy but dreadful in politics". It is a paradox too difficult to justify, yet it has deceived too many people in Hong Kong.

My second question: Can Hong Kong break away from China?

Hong Kong has been part of China from time immemorial, and became a special administrative region after the reunification. It is preposterous and nonsensical to say that Hong Kong people are not Chinese. One may leave Hong Kong and migrate to another country, but body features like dark hair and yellow skin are innate qualities that cannot be altered. Whether they like it or not, as long as they live in Hong Kong, most of the water, electricity, meat and vegetables are from the northern hinterland. Wherever they travel to, as long as they possess an SAR passport, the Chinese embassy is the only place they can seek help when problems arise.

A country can only have one sovereign power, and Hong Kong is inseparable from the State. Those who marched with the American and British flags probably wished foreign governments would protect them and govern Hong Kong. But China is no longer the one that was subject to arbitrary oppression in contemporary history; the central government in Beijing and the 1.4 billion Chinese people will not permit any act that brings disgrace and humiliation upon our country again!

My third question: Do you see the future of China?

In the past 70 years, Chinese people have stood up; our country has become prosperous and is becoming stronger. China's development blueprint of becoming a strong, democratic, civilized, harmonious and beautiful socialist modern nation by the middle of this century has already been outlined. The timing precisely coincides with the 50-year deadline of "one country, two systems". The "two systems" complement each other and allow Hong Kong and the motherland to share mutual glory. China's development is inexorable, and it is just a matter of time before the nation becomes the biggest economy in the world. This prospect is not pie in the sky. The institutional advantages and the abundant experiences China enjoys, synergized with the solidarity of 1.4 billion citizens, will eventually turn the Chinese dream into reality.

It is not surprising that some people do not see these bright prospects. To date, "theories" such as "the end of history" and "collapse of China" are still lingering in our ears. Chinese citizens are no longer abused nor starved, yet insults are still hurled at us simply because the world's mainstream media and opinion are controlled by the West. China is reproached because it has embarked on a path different from that of the West. Consequently, no matter how many good deeds the Communist Party of China has done for the Chinese people and the international community, it will still be repeatedly bashed and treated as a nonconformist. China does not intend to export its political system; it is only that we have found a path of development that suits us, and we are determined to continue with this path. The world is undergoing great changes unseen in a century, with a focus on competition among political systems, of which China is not afraid. Seventy years of vicissitudes have given us much confidence to look forward to a bright future!

Credit: October 31, 2019, *Wen Wei Po*

November 4, 2019, *China Daily Hong Kong*